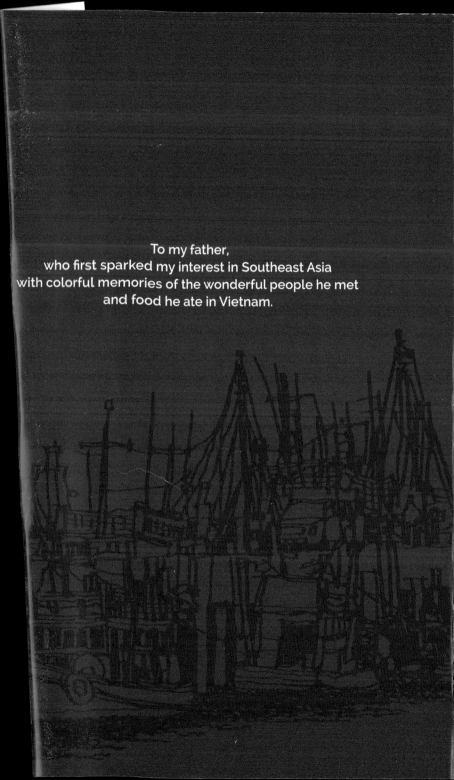

To my father,
who first sparked my interest in Southeast Asia
with colorful memories of the wonderful people he met
and food he ate in Vietnam.

THE
FISH SAU
COOKBO

THE
FISH SAUCE
COOKBOOK

50 Umami-Packed Recipes from Around the Globe

VERONICA MEEWES

Photography by Clare Barboza

Andrews McMeel
Publishing®

Kansas City • Sydney • London

CONTENTS

INTRODUCTION | ix

MAKING FISH SAUCE AT HOME | 1
    Vegan Nước Chấm   2
    Homemade Fish Sauce   4

SAUCES MADE WITH FISH SAUCE | 5
    Caramel Miso Glaze   6
    Rappahannock Mignonette   7
    Apple Relish   8
    Fish Sauce Béarnaise   9
    MoPho-Style Barbecue Shrimp Sauce   10

SOUPS AND SALADS | 13
    Thai Hot and Sour Coconut Chicken Soup   14
    Seafood Chowder with Thai Flavors   16
    Kimchi Stew with Tuna and Ramen Noodles   19
    Crab and Roasted Tomato Soup in Spicy Garlic Ginger Broth   22
    Kale Caesar Salad with Spiedini Croutons   23
    Chicken and Candied Shrimp Salad   26
    Braised Duck with Ginger Lime Slaw   28
    Green Mango, Sorrel, and Candied Pecans in Spicy Palm Sugar Syrup   30

SMALL BITES | 31

Sweet and Spicy Caramel Corn with Cashews and Fish Sauce Caramel   32

Crispy Pork Steam Buns with Fish Sauce Vinaigrette   34

Shrimp Toast with Nước Chấm   36

Vietnamese Meatballs   39

Crab Fat Wings   41

Shrimp and Pork Belly Bánh Mì   42

VEGETABLE SIDES | 43

Crispy Farmer's Market Vegetables with Caramelized Fish Sauce   44

Korean Pikliz   45

Warm Brussels Sprout Slaw with Asian Citrus Dressing   47

Shaved Winter Squash   48

Wood Roasted Summer Squash with Palm Sugar, Soy,
and Fish Sauce Vinaigrette   50

Skillet Greens, Crisp Shallots, Nước Mắm Apple Cider Gastrique   52

PASTA | 53

Late Summer Pasta Sauce   54

Ode to Sardella   56

MEAT ENTRÉES | 59

Vietnamese Caramel Chicken   60

Spice-Lacquered Duck Breasts, Baby Turnips, and Turnip Greens   61

Fermented Pork and Rice Sausage, Larb Salad, and Fish Sauce Vinaigrette   64

Marinated Grilled Short Rib with Anchovy Salad, Green Tomato Jam,
and Sweet Potato Purée   66

Freedmen's Pulled Pork   69

Mustard and Beer-Braised Brisket   70

Thit Kho Caramelized Braised Pork Belly and Eggs   72

SEAFOOD ENTRÉES | 75

Hamachi Tostada with Fish Sauce Vinaigrette   77
Grilled Peaches, Crispy Maine Shrimp, Chiles, and Herbs   79
Steamed Dover Sole with Fried Chopped Radish in Soya Sauce   80
Blue Crab Fried Rice with Nam Phrik Pla   82
Rice-Seared Red Trout with Mandarin and Hazelnut Brown Butter   85
Halibut with Browned Butter, Lemon, and Aged Fish Sauce   86
Lobster with Fish Sauce Caramel   87
Mussels in Coconut Chili Broth   88
Zucchini Tofu Shrimp Frittata with Fish Sauce   90

COCKTAILS | 91

Fish Sauce Bloody Mary   93
Hanoi High Five   94
Saigon Shrub   96

DESSERT | 97

Coconut Buddha's Hand Sundae with Fish Sauce Latik   98
Apple Fritters with Fish Sauce Apple Marmalade   102

Contributor Biographies   105
Metric Conversions and Equivalents   119
Index   121

INTRODUCTION

When I began telling people I was working on this cookbook, most of the reactions I received were versions of the same sentiment: "I've had the same bottle of fish sauce in my pantry forever, and I just don't know what to do with it!"

Hopefully, this collection of fifty recipes, contributed by renowned chefs and passionate food writers, helps to demystify the funky condiment that's been popping up on menus all over the country lately. Using this as your guide, you'll soon find that fish sauce is not only a staple of Asian cuisine, but surprisingly can be utilized in everything from Evan LeRoy's Freedmen's Pulled Pork on page 69 to cocktails like Lara Nixon's Saigon Shrub on page 96 to desserts like Andrew Lewis's Apple Fritters with Fish Sauce Apple Marmalade on page 102.

Straight from the bottle, the intense fishy aroma can be off-putting for some home cooks. But when used in moderation, fish sauce can add great flavor undertones to a dish—without necessarily smelling or tasting like it crawled out of the ocean.

You see, fish sauce is the epitome of umami, the fifth taste that occurs when the amino acid glutamate is present. Appropriately named after the Japanese word for "delicious," umami can be found in rich stocks, savory dashi (Japanese stocks), and earthy mushrooms. Fermentation helps unleash umami flavors, which are prevalent in products like soy sauce, cured meats, aged cheeses, and fish sauce.

"It's this brilliant way of layering in flavor complexities," explains fermentation expert Sandor Katz. "And I think in the world of fermented condiments there's quite a few examples of things that actually taste a little bit nasty in their pure form, but they really do serve to introduce incredible flavor complexities when you use just a little bit in a big dish."

THE HISTORY OF FISH SAUCE

Though Dr. Kikunae Ikeda of Japan defined umami in the early 1900s, it didn't start to be recognized as the fifth taste until the 1980s. But humans have been craving that savory flavor for much longer than that. In fact, the first accounts of fish sauce fermentation actually date back to ancient Rome, where *garum* was created from anchovies, sardines, mackerel, or tuna, which were salted and left in the sun to ferment for several months. They were then strained and often fortified with honey, wine, herbs, or vinegar.

Ryan Pera, chef-owner of Coltivare in Houston, discovered *garum* while reading Apicius in college. The collection of ancient Roman recipes, which is thought to be one of the earliest printed cookbooks, dates back to the late fourth and early fifth century AD. Chicago chef Chris Pandel also became intrigued with the ancient ingredient and even re-created many of the original Roman recipes for a special dinner at his restaurant Balena.

These days, the closest thing to *garum* on the market is *colatura di alici*, a salted anchovy liquid crafted on Italy's Amalfi coast and aged in oak barrels for three to four years. A 3- to 4-ounce bottle of the stuff can run between $20 and $30, but for good reason. Unlike Southeast Asian fish sauces that are diluted by about 20 percent when bottled, *colatura di alici* is highly concentrated. That means a little goes a long way. Though the substance smells intensely fishy when first opened, using just a little bit will lend that elusive je ne sais quoi to your dish. Try it in a salad dressing such as the Kale Caesar Salad with Spiedini Croutons (page 23), or toss it with pasta, olive oil, garlic, and red pepper. Gerard Craft's Ode to Sardella on page 56 is a zesty pasta dish that can use either fish sauce or *colatura*.

While Pera and Pandel primarily use Asian-style fish sauce in their kitchens, they incorporate *colatura* in sauces or drizzled atop a dish in lieu of a balsamic reduction. "We reserve the *colatura* as a finishing agent in our kitchens almost like a single-press olive oil or a finishing sea salt," explains Pandel.

HOW FISH SAUCE IS MADE

Interestingly enough, fish sauce didn't make its way down to Asia until about 1,000 years after it was documented in Italy. Some speculate that it was passed along the trade route known as the Silk Road, though it is entirely possible that Asian fish sauce was created independently of the brine Italians were simmering. In the East, anchovies were incorporated, instead of the tuna and mackerel available in the Mediterranean, and the

condiment began to morph into the modern "clear" Asian fish sauce we know and use today.

The process for making fish sauce hasn't changed much through the years. Much like *garum*, fresh fish are salted and layered in barrels or clay pits, then left to ferment in the heat of the sun for up to a year. Bricks or bamboo mats press down on the fish as its digestive enzymes break down the flesh, resulting in fermentation.

"If you took fillets of fish and tried to make fish sauce out of that, it probably wouldn't work," explains fermentation expert Sandor Katz. "The intestines are critical to the process. That's the source of the bacteria. So it's just fish, a lot of salt, a little bit of weight bearing down on it, and patience."

Next, the liquid is drained out of the vats. Much like a fine olive oil, the first "press" is the highest quality (though it is more of a first "drain"). Some companies will then age the strained liquid for another several months; the longer it sits, the lighter and sweeter it becomes. "The idea is, over a length of time, it develops secondary and tertiary flavors that aren't just rotten fish," explains Todd Duplechan, chef/owner of Lenoir in Austin, who also has his own batch of fish sauce currently fermenting.

"The thing with doing it yourself at home is sometimes you'll be like, 'This is great!' and other times it won't be as good," says Duplechan. "There are so many different factors— it was too hot, it wasn't hot enough, the type of fish, what the fish were eating, where they were from—it's endless." On pages 2 and 4, you'll find recipes for making your own fish sauce at home. But if you don't have nine to twelve months to wait, there are plenty of brands out there from which to choose.

HOW TO SELECT A FISH SAUCE

Perusing the fish sauce aisle of the Asian market can indeed be an intimidating experience. A rainbow of labels line the shelves, typically written in unfamiliar languages. Some specimens are dark and translucent, while others are lighter in color but thick and viscous. Where to begin?

First, read the label. The best sauces will be made from just one type of fish (anchovy is most common) rather than a blend. There also shouldn't be many other ingredients listed; traditionally, fish sauce is made from just fish and salt. If there are a slew of unpronounceable preservatives and additives on the ingredient list (i.e., MSG or artificial sweeteners), move along.

Some bottles will have the nitrogen content listed as "degrees N." The degrees refer to the amount of nitrogen per liter, which is a measure of the sauce's intensity and protein level. A 30°N is standard, so anything higher is more concentrated and incrementally more expensive.

Brands of Fish Sauce

Many different Asian cultures have their own version of fish sauce. In Vietnam it's known as *nước mắm* and, in Thailand, *nam pla*. In Japan it's called *shottsuru*, Korea has *aek jeot*, the Phillippines has *patis,* and Cambodians call theirs *prahoc*. Vietnamese and Thai fish sauces are by far the most ubiquitous in Asian markets, with the former known for being more nuanced and delicate in flavor.

Some of the best fish sauce in the world is said to come from Phu Quoc, an island in Vietnam. That's where Red Boat produces their popular 40°N and 50°N varieties. Though a favorite among chefs for their pure, clean flavor and briny minerality, these premium sauces are definitely some of the most expensive on the market ($6.95 to $8 a bottle), making them less realistic for most restaurants to buy in bulk. Red Boat has also collaborated with BLiS to produce a fish sauce that is aged for seven months in Kentucky bourbon barrels. The result is smoky, complex, and in a class of its own.

Viet Huong Fish Sauce Company produces a variety of different fish sauces, from the sweet and almost crabby Three Crabs (which, ironically, is made using only anchovies) to its lighter counterparts One Crab and the more intense Five Crabs. And, while there is no Four Crabs, they do produce a Flying Lion variety that is full-flavored and medium bodied. Viet Huong actually has facilities on Phu Quoc Island, as well as in Thailand, and they blend the sauce from both regions before bottling it in their Hong Kong facility.

Other Thai varieties of fish sauce include Tiparos, which is quite salty before its sweet aftertaste and certainly the best value, retailing at around $2 a bottle. Squid is also quite intensely briny and pungent, and Flying Lion is quite similar to an earthy, concentrated soy sauce. While notably bolder than Vietnamese fish sauce, these varieties are a good match for the dynamic flavors found in Thai cuisine.

Megachef makes a 30°N premium fish sauce that is produced in Thailand, but less fishy and salty than most Thai varieties. Added sugar gives it a sweeter, slightly floral undertone, and it smells of porcini mushrooms rather than fish. Almost all of the varieties listed here are recommended by chefs throughout this book, so the brand you choose is just really a matter of personal preference.

PROPER STORAGE

The high salt content of fish sauce acts as a preservative by inhibiting microbial growth and preventing spoilage. So, while fish sauce may be stored at room temperature, keep in mind that it is still subject to oxidation, much like wine. Its freshness and true flavor will last longest in the refrigerator. However, fish sauces with added sugar will begin to crystallize when refrigerated, in which case a cool pantry (75 to 80°F) will also work. Most bottles will have a "best before" date, but using it within a year is a good guideline.

Once you begin cooking with fish sauce more regularly, you'll become more familiar with how it should look, smell, and taste. While a fishy smell is normal, a completely rotten, putrid smell is not. A translucent amber color is ideal, though different brands vary in lightness, akin to tea in different stages of steeping. If you notice it becoming darker or forming salt crystals or mold, immediately discard the bottle.

VIETNAMESE FISH SAUCE TERMINOLOGY

You'll notice several similar-looking fish sauce phrases used in Vietnamese recipes (including a few in this book). When dining in a Vietnamese restaurant, ask your server for *nước mắm,* and you will typically receive fish sauce for dipping. Or your server might ask you to clarify whether you'd like dipping fish sauce (*nước mắm pha*) or pure fish sauce (*nước mắm nguyên chất*). As a guide:

Nước chấm refers to any general dipping sauce or condiment.

Nước mắm is the colloquial term used for the pure fish sauce as well as the dipping sauce condiment.

Nước mắm pha (*pha* means mixed) specifically refers to fish sauce mixed with other ingredients and intended for dipping.

Nước mắm nguyên chất (*nguyên chất* means pure) specifically denotes fish sauce straight from the bottle.

THE BLOOD OF VIETNAMESE COOKING

Los Angeles–based chef Connie Tran's memories of fish sauce date back to the last few years of the Vietnam War when her father, a lieutenant colonel in the military, would return home to Saigon to share a meal with his family.

"My mother always prepared amazing suppers that exemplified the cornerstones of balance in a Vietnamese meal," she recalls, "centering around a bowl of *nước chấm* made up of fish sauce, fresh lime juice, lime supremes, and slices of fresh red chiles floating to the top." The *nước chấm* was served with traditional accompaniments: a broth or clear soup, a cooked or raw vegetable dish, and a small meat or fish dish intentionally oversalted to promote the eating of more steamed rice.

"Fish sauce is the blood of Vietnamese cooking," says Tran. "It defines not only the Vietnamese people's culinary identity, within the nation and diaspora, but also Vietnam's geography, economy, and history."

As a first-generation Vietnamese immigrant, she remembers how foreign the smell and sight of her fish sauce–braised pork and rice must have appeared to her American peers eating peanut butter and jelly for lunch.

"Now I wonder about how the Vietnamese American cultural identity will evolve, and what fish sauce and the craft of making, cooking, and eating it will look like with future generations," Tran muses. "Fish sauce takes time to get ready for the world, and a little goes a long way. So, in a sense, what we make today will be ready for future generations, so that guarantees a bit of our cultural identity for a while!"

We wish you many exciting new culinary experiences with this liquid gift from the sea!

This cookbook came to be thanks to the often family-run companies who've kept the tradition of handcrafted fish sauce alive, as well as the inspired work of the many talented chefs who contributed recipes. We are paying it forward by donating a portion of the proceeds to the MilkCare Foundation (milkcare.org). This 501(c)(3) volunteer-run nonprofit organization serves abandoned, homeless, and underprivileged children in Vietnam.

Until economic reforms in 1986, the Vietnamese government provided free schooling. Now, many disenfranchised families cannot afford to provide their children with basic nutrition or an education. MilkCare Foundation provides schools and orphanages with a soybean milk program, necessities like food and clothing, a scholarship program from primary to college level students, and financial support to assist with teachers' salaries and school improvement. They have provided eighty-seven college scholarships, twenty-five high school scholarships, and seven junior high scholarships to children from eight different cities in Vietnam in recent years.

MAKING
FISH SAUCE
AT HOME

MAM NEM

INGREDIENT : FISH, SALT, WATER
THÀNH PHẦN : CÁ CƠM, MUỐI, NƯỚC

DISTRIBUTOR
IHA BEVERAGE
COMMERCE CA.90040
FL.OZ.(207ML)

Chef Connie Tran was born in Nha Trang, Vietnam, into a large family in which food was always a focus. "I was raised on fish sauce, as it is ubiquitous in Vietnamese cuisine," she says. "There was probably fish sauce in my baby formula!" These days, she's garnered much attention throughout the Los Angeles area for her BEP Vietnamese Kitchen pop-up events, which always sell out quickly. She developed this vegan version of *nước chấm* so that her Buddhist and vegan friends, family, and customers can enjoy otherwise vegetarian dishes that call for fish sauce. "It can be used anywhere the condiment *nước chấm* is called for or as a marinade. My favorite way is using it for salad dressing." She notes that while the fresh lime juice is essential, light brown sugar may be substituted for palm sugar, which comes either loose or packaged in cakes that can be grated with a Microplane or similarly sharp grater.

VEGAN NƯỚC CHẤM

Chef/Owner **CONNIE TRAN** | **BEP VIETNAMESE KITCHEN** Los Angeles, California

3 tablespoons palm sugar

2 cups low-sodium vegetable broth

1 teaspoon sea salt

1 tablespoon freshly squeezed lime juice

½ teaspoon sambal chili paste

½ teaspoon grated fresh ginger

½ teaspoon grated garlic

Grate the palm sugar (if necessary) and put it into a small pot. Add the vegetable broth and heat over medium-low heat until the sugar has dissolved and the mixture has reduced to half its original volume. Remove from the heat and let cool to room temperature. Add the salt and lime juice and stir until the salt has dissolved. Add the sambal, ginger, and garlic. The sauce can be kept for up to 3 days in the refrigerator but it's best to serve it immediately, before the lime juice begins to lose its bright citrus flavor.

MAKES 1 CUP

Kresha Faber's website *Nourishing Joy* celebrates all things DIY, with recipes for everything from bath and beauty products to natural home remedies to homemade versions of foods like string cheese or Cheerios. Though an entire section of her site is dedicated to fermented foods, it wasn't until recently that she attempted her own fish sauce. "In the wide, wonderful world of fermentation, homemade fish sauce was one of those foods I just couldn't fathom making at home," she says. "But fast-forward a few weeks when I opened that first jar of homemade fish sauce and took a brave little taste—and it was *good*. Its flavor was complex but by no means overwhelming. It was barely fishy and it was bursting with umami." While commercial fish sauces are typically fermented for six months to a year, this is a quicker version for the home cook.

HOMEMADE
FISH SAUCE

KRESHA FABER | author of *The DIY Pantry* and editor of **NOURISHINGJOY.COM**

6 cloves garlic, coarsely
   chopped

Finely grated zest of
   1 small lemon (optional)

3 tablespoons fine sea salt

1½ pounds small whole fish
   (smelt, herring, etc.)

2 to 3 teaspoons whole black
   peppercorns

6 bay leaves

2 tablespoons sauerkraut
   brine, fresh whey, or
   1 teaspoon additional
   sea salt

1 to 2 cups nonchlorinated
   water, as needed

Muddle the garlic and the lemon zest together with the sea salt in a medium bowl. Rinse the fish, then cut it into ½-inch pieces. Toss the fish pieces (including the heads and tails) in the muddled salt mixture to completely coat the fish. Add the peppercorns and bay leaves, then lightly pack the mixture into a clean 1-quart Mason jar, pressing down on the pieces as you go to release the juices.

Pour the sauerkraut brine into the jar, then pour in as much water as needed to completely submerge the fish, but leaving at least 1 inch of headspace at the top of the jar, as the mixture will expand as it ferments.

Cover tightly and leave at room temperature for 2 to 3 days, then move to the refrigerator and let sit for 4 to 6 weeks, depending on taste preference. (The fish sauce should actually smooth out in flavor the longer it sits.) Strain the mixture twice through a fine sieve or cheesecloth and discard the solids. Store in glass bottles in the refrigerator for 4 to 6 months.

MAKES ABOUT 1¾ CUPS

MẮM NÊM THÁI

U-DO SAUCE

'QUID BRAND
SH SAUCE

GREDIENTS:
Extract, Salt, Sugar.

oduct contains
sh (Anchovy)

ET HUONG FISHSAUCE COMPAN

THREE CRABS Bran

SAUCES
MADE WITH FISH SAUCE

908

SAUCE
(ALAYAN)
AQUEREAU

幸福

善別香甜魚製

Cơm Ăn Liề

Chef Monica Pope's Cooking Therapy classes, held upstairs at her restaurant Sparrow Bar + Cookshop, offer her favorite recipes, techniques, and ingredients gathered over twenty years of professional cooking. One of her favorites is this caramel miso glaze, which she uses over her crispy Brussels sprouts or serves with cuts of steak in conjunction with her Blossom Butter, a compound butter made with herbs, edible flowers, lemon zest, and salt and pepper. According to Pope, it's "fat on fat on fat, I love to say—so good!"

CARAMEL MISO
GLAZE

Chef/Owner **MONICA POPE** | **SPARROW BAR • COOKSHOP** Houston, Texas

2 cups sugar

1¼ cups (2½ sticks) unsalted butter, divided

4 teaspoons minced garlic

¼ cup minced shallots

Sea salt and cracked black pepper

2 cups pork or chicken stock

½ cup shiro (white) miso

¾ cup red wine vinegar

¼ cup soy sauce

¼ cup fish sauce

Make the caramel sauce by placing the sugar and 1 tablespoon water in a saucepan and cook over medium heat until dark amber. Add 1 cup of the butter and stir until melted. Remove from the heat.

Sauté the garlic and shallots in the remaining ¼ cup butter in a large saucepan over medium heat until clear or translucent. Season with a pinch of salt and pepper. Add the stock, caramel sauce, miso, vinegar, soy sauce, and fish sauce. Bring to a simmer over low heat for 30 seconds and then remove from the heat. Use immediately or store in the refrigerator in a glass container for up to 2 weeks. Bring to a boil to reheat and serve over vegetables, steak, or fish.

MAKES 4 CUPS

Before opening Rappahannock in Richmond, Executive Chef Dylan Fultineer had developed a homemade barrel-aged red wine vinegar to use as the base of its house mignonette. Upon realizing how difficult it was to keep up with production, he decided to switch to regular red wine vinegar while adding fish sauce for complexity. "Fish sauce is a tool, much like salt or anchovies, that can be used to season food," says Fultineer. "It adds an incredible savory element that you can't get from just adding salt. We use it much like you would an anchovy. Fish sauce adds depth, salt, and savory, but doesn't come off as fishy when used in the right quantity." This mignonette is wonderful served with oysters on the half shell.

RAPPAHANNOCK
MIGNONETTE

Executive Chef **DYLAN FULTINEER** | **RAPPAHANNOCK** Richmond, Virginia

2 shallots, minced

1 cup red wine vinegar

1 tablespoon sugar

¼ cup fish sauce

1 tablespoon cracked black pepper

Oysters on the half shell, for serving

Fresh horseradish, for serving

Lemon wedges, for serving

Combine the shallots, vinegar, sugar, fish sauce, pepper, and 1 cup water in a bowl. Stir well and serve with trays of oysters on the half shell, fresh horseradish, and lemon wedges. The mignonette may be made ahead of time and stored in a sealed container in the refrigerator for up to a week.

MAKES ABOUT 2½ CUPS

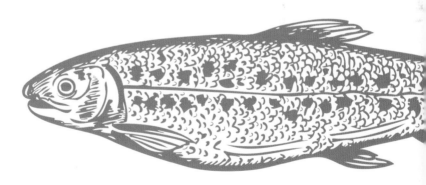

Chef Stephanie Izard is so enamored by fish sauce that she recently wrote the ingredient a love letter for *Esquire* magazine. "I love fish sauce and I have to hold myself back from using it on everything on the menu!" she says. "It's a great way to add flavor so simply and it's freakin' delicious!" You'll find it in the aioli accompanying her green beans at Girl & the Goat, or as a main ingredient in her addictive bottled Sauté sauce. Her kitchen staff goes through container after container of Three Crabs—a brand that, despite its name, is shellfish-free. These days, the sweet, salty, and tangy combination of malt vinegar and fish sauce is a particular favorite of hers. This relish once appeared on a turkey sandwich in the Little Goat deli, but Izard recommends using it to spice up any meat or fish dish.

APPLE RELISH

Chef/Owner **STEPHANIE IZARD** | **LITTLE GOAT** Chicago, Illinois

3 tablespoons canola oil, divided

2 red apples, peeled, cored, and thinly sliced

3 tablespoons fish sauce, divided

3 tablespoons malt vinegar, divided

Salt

1 medium red onion, thinly sliced (to same thickness as the apples)

2 cups beech mushrooms, trimmed

Heat 1 tablespoon of the canola oil in a sauté pan over medium-low heat. Add the apples and sauté until tender, 2 to 3 minutes. Add 1 tablespoon of the fish sauce and 1 tablespoon of the malt vinegar. Toss to combine. Season with salt, remove from the pan, and set aside.

Heat 1 tablespoon of the canola oil in the same sauté pan over medium-low heat. Add the onion and sauté until tender, 2 to 3 minutes. Add 1 tablespoon of the fish sauce and 1 tablespoon of the malt vinegar. Toss to combine. Season with salt, remove from the pan, and set aside.

Heat the remaining 1 tablespoon canola oil in the same pan over medium-low heat. Add the mushrooms and sauté until tender, 2 to 3 minutes. Add the remaining 1 tablespoon fish sauce and remaining 1 tablespoon malt vinegar. Toss to combine. Season with salt, remove from the pan, and set aside.

Combine the apples, red onion, and mushrooms in a bowl. Stir together and serve at room temperature.

SERVES 4

In this spin on a traditional Béarnaise sauce, Chef Jeremy Lieb replaces some of the acid with fish sauce and the cayenne with chili oil. "The splash of fermented fish adds funk and umami to the egg rich emulsion," says Lieb. He recommends adding chopped cilantro and citrus zest when serving it with fish, or adding chopped tomato and fine herbs when it accompanies grilled meats. "Or there's my personal favorite," he says. "Simply lather it onto crispy french fries and serve with crisp champagne. Anyway you dip it, it's delicious." Squid is Lieb's preferred brand of fish sauce.

FISH SAUCE
BÉARNAISE

Executive Chef **JEREMY LIEB** | **BOCA** Cincinnati, Ohio

TARRAGON VINEGAR REDUCTION

4½ cups tarragon vinegar

2 shallots, finely chopped

2 tablespoons dried tarragon

BÉARNAISE

9 egg yolks

1 quart clarified butter, warm

4 ounces fish sauce

4 ounces freshly squeezed lemon juice

2 ounces chili oil

Fresh herbs of your choice, finely chopped

To make the tarragon vinegar reduction, combine the vinegar, shallots, and tarragon in a saucepan and simmer over low heat. Cook until the mixture has reduced to 1½ cups. Strain the reduction using a fine-mesh strainer and set aside to use in the Béarnaise. Keep warm.

To make the Béarnaise, add ½ ounce tepid water to the egg yolks and whisk together in the top of a double boiler over low heat until thickened. Remove from the heat and slowly add one-quarter of the warm vinegar reduction. Next, slowly add half the warm butter followed by half the remaining vinegar reduction, all while whisking vigorously. Slowly add the remaining butter while continuing to whisk. Add the remaining vinegar reduction, then add the fish sauce and whisk. Add the lemon juice and whisk, then add the chili oil and whisk. Season with fresh herbs of your choosing and serve with fish, grilled meats, or potatoes. The sauce may be stored in an airtight container in the refrigerator for up to a month. Bring to a simmer to reheat before using.

MAKES 2 QUARTS

At MoPho in New Orleans, Chef Michael Gulotta marries the bold flavors of Southeast Asia with New Orleans bounty and Cajun soul. This dish is based on a childhood memory of his stepfather shrimping with firefighter friends each shrimp season. "His payment would be in big beautiful Louisiana shrimp," remembers Gulotta. "Much of the shrimp would be boiled or fried, but the highlight was always barbecued shrimp served with lots of crusty French bread for sopping up the sauce. This is a sauce we originally came up with to serve over big head-on shrimp we grilled in our outdoor fire pit. We found that the addition of the fish sauce deepened the flavor and brought a complexity and brininess that shellfish stock alone could not."

MOPHO-STYLE
BARBECUE SHRIMP SAUCE

Chef/Partner **MICHAEL GULOTTA** | **MOPHO** New Orleans, Louisiana

1 head garlic

1 tablespoon neutral oil

1 cup (2 sticks) unsalted butter

1 tablespoon minced fresh ginger

1 cup shellfish stock

1 cup heavy cream

1 cup unsweetened coconut milk

3 tablespoons fish sauce

3 tablespoons Worcestershire sauce

2 teaspoons paprika

1 tablespoon Sichuan peppercorns, ground

Juice of 1 lemon

Finely grated zest of 1 lime

¼ teaspoon cayenne

1 sprig fresh thyme

Salt

Broiled or grilled shrimp, for serving

Finely chopped fresh flat-leaf parsley or thinly sliced scallions, for garnish

Preheat the oven to 375°F. Cut just the root off the head of garlic, exposing the bottom of all the cloves. Rub the head with oil, wrap it in aluminum foil, and roast for 30 minutes, or until tender. Let cool and then remove the cloves from their peel and reserve.

In a medium saucepan over medium-high heat, melt the butter and bring to a boil. Once the butter begins to froth at the top and smells of toasted nuts, remove the pan from the heat and stir the browning butter with a spoon, being careful not to splash. Add the ginger and roasted garlic cloves to the hot butter. Return the pan to the heat, stir, and allow to toast for 1 minute.

Add the shellfish stock, cream, and coconut milk, then place the mixture back over medium heat and bring to a simmer. Once the sauce begins to simmer, stir in the fish sauce, Worcestershire, paprika, peppercorns, lemon juice, lime zest, cayenne, and thyme.

Continued

Remove the pan from the heat and allow the flavors to steep for 5 minutes. Remove the thyme sprig from the sauce and discard. Carefully pour the sauce into a blender and purée on low until the roasted garlic cloves are well incorporated. Season with salt to taste and serve warm over sautéed, broiled, or grilled Louisiana shrimp. Garnish with parsley or green onion. The sauce may be kept in an airtight container in the refrigerator for up to 1 week. Reheat in a heavy-bottomed saucepan over medium heat before serving.

MAKES 4 CUPS

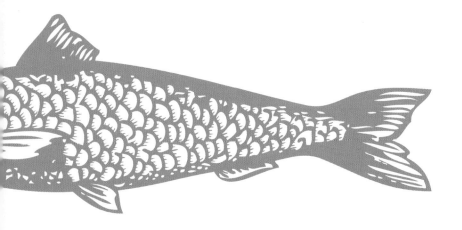

MAM NEM
INGREDIENT : FISH, SALT, WATER
THÀNH PHẦN : CÁ CƠM, MUỐI, NƯỚC

DISTRIBUTOR
IHA BEVERAGE
COMMERCE CA.90040
NET 7 FL.OZ.(207ML)
LOT NO 13.013.01
PRODUCT OF VIETNAM

SAUCE
(ALAYAN)
QUEREAU

SOUPS
AND
SALADS

(GRADE A) STEA

KIML

'quic
BRAND
SH SAUCE

GREDIENTS:
Extract, Salt, Sugar.
roduct contains
sh (Anchovy)

Sauce
Phan Thiết

This take on a classic Thai dish, hot and sour coconut chicken soup *(tom kha gai)*, is comforting, flavorful, and one of Chef Andrew Zimmern's favorite dishes to make for visiting guests. Though effortless to prepare, this soup doesn't skimp on bold flavor. "The fish sauce in this recipe supplies the stalwart salt component and fermented umami blast so critical to making this soup perfectly balanced," says Zimmern. "That balance is at the very core of what Thai cookery is all about. Maximalist flavor and devout composition of sour, salty, bitter and sweet—not minimalist in any way."

THAI HOT AND SOUR
COCONUT CHICKEN SOUP

Celebrity Chef **ANDREW ZIMMERN** | Minneapolis, Minnesota

1 pound skinless, boneless chicken thighs, sliced crosswise into 2 by ¼-inch pieces

¼ cup fish sauce

3 cups low-sodium chicken stock or broth

2½ tablespoons light brown sugar

1 tablespoon plus 2 teaspoons Thai red chili paste

1 tablespoon plus 1 teaspoon tamarind concentrate

1 tablespoon finely grated fresh ginger

2 tablespoons minced lemongrass, tender white part only

2 fresh or dried kaffir lime leaves, or 1 teaspoon finely grated lime zest

2 (14-ounce) cans coconut milk

½ pound shiitake mushrooms, stemmed, caps thinly sliced

¼ cup freshly squeezed lime juice

2 red or green Thai chiles, very thinly sliced on an angle

⅓ cup packed fresh cilantro leaves, for garnish

In a medium bowl, toss the chicken with the fish sauce. Set aside.

In a large pot, combine the stock with the sugar, chili paste, tamarind, ginger, lemongrass, and lime leaves and bring to a boil over medium-high heat. Stir in the coconut milk and bring to a simmer. Add the chicken and fish sauce along with the mushrooms and simmer, stirring occasionally, until the chicken is cooked through and the mushrooms are tender, about 3 minutes.

Remove from the heat and discard the lime leaves. Stir in the lime juice and chiles. Ladle the soup into bowls, then sprinkle with the cilantro and serve.

SERVES 6 TO 8 AS A MAIN COURSE

As one of the leading authorities on New England cuisine, Chef Jasper White has been studying and experimenting with chowder for years. "Chowder is a dish that has been evolving for over 300 years," he says. "Until fifty years ago, it was always made as a main course, not a soup. It has always featured common local ingredients, and as different ingredients became available, they made their way into the chowder pot." This Southeast Asian interpretation was inspired by a soup made by runner-up Gregory Gourdet on an episode of *Top Chef* season twelve, on which White served as the judge. "This recipe is made in the spirit of chowder, and although the flavors are somewhat unusual, it might be viewed as part of the evolution of this ancient dish," explains White. He stresses that the curing of the chowder (letting it rest after it is finished) is the most important step in the process. While forty minutes is the minimum time required for the flavors to meld, it can actually be made up to a day or two before serving.

SEAFOOD CHOWDER
WITH THAI FLAVORS

Chef/Owner **JASPER WHITE** | **SUMMER SHACK** Cambridge

SEAFOOD

3 pounds cherrystone clams (about 10)

1 pound medium shrimp (26 to 30 count)

1 pound squid, cleaned, cut into rings, and tentacles cut down to size

BROTH

1 large yellow onion (10 ounces), thinly sliced

2 ounces fresh ginger, peeled and coarsely chopped

6 cloves garlic, thinly sliced

1 stalk lemongrass, coarsely chopped

2 cups tomatoes in juice, fresh or canned

3 tablespoons Thai yellow curry paste

⅓ cup fish sauce

4 cups fish or chicken stock

CHOWDER

¼ cup vegetable oil

1 medium green bell pepper, seeded and cut into medium dice

1 medium red bell pepper, seeded and cut into medium dice

1 large yellow onion (10 ounces), cut into medium dice

3 small carrots (3 ounces), cut into ¼-inch-thick rounds

Bottled clam juice (optional)

2 medium sweet potatoes (24 ounces), peeled and cut into medium dice

1 green (unripened) papaya, peeled, seeded, and cut into medium dice

1 (13-ounce) can unsweetened coconut milk

Juice of 2 limes

3 sprigs fresh mint, leaves chopped

3 sprigs fresh Thai basil, leaves chopped

Salt and freshly ground black pepper

Fish sauce (optional)

Jasmine rice, for serving

Continued

To prep the seafood, first scrub and rinse the clams. Place them in a small pot with a tight-fitting lid and add 1 cup water. Place over high heat and steam the clams until they open, 8 to 10 minutes. Discard any clams that do not open. Strain the steaming broth with a basket strainer and reserve about 2 cups. Dice the clam meat and set them aside. Peel and devein the shrimp, reserving the shells for the broth.

To make the broth, place the reserved shrimp shells, onion, ginger, garlic, lemongrass, tomatoes, curry paste, fish sauce, stock, and 2 cups water in a medium stockpot and bring to a boil over medium-high heat. Decrease the heat to low and simmer for about 30 minutes. Strain the shellfish broth through a fine-mesh strainer, yielding about 6 cups. Set aside.

To make the chowder, combine the oil, peppers, onion, and carrots in a large soup pot (6 quarts). Sauté over medium-high heat until the vegetables are tender, 8 minutes. Add the shellfish broth, reserved clam steaming water (if you don't have quite 2 cups, you can add a little bottled clam juice or water), sweet potatoes, and papaya. Bring to a boil, then lower the heat and simmer until the potatoes are tender, 8 to 10 minutes. Add the coconut milk and shrimp. Cook for 1 minute longer and turn off the heat. Add the squid and chopped clams, then let the mixture sit for at least 40 minutes.

Reheat gently over low heat and add the lime juice along with the mint and basil. Season to taste with pepper and more fish sauce or salt, if desired. Serve as a main course in soup plates with bowls of jasmine rice on the side.

SERVES 6 TO 8 AS A MAIN COURSE

Chef Jack Gilmore began cooking on the Gulf coast in 1975. Having studied under Cajun chefs on South Padre Island and worked in the bayous of Louisiana, he's no stranger to the ocean's bounty. In Austin, he's known for flavorful dishes made with the best local ingredients and products, and on a recent trip to the Bahamas, he employed the same practices. All the ingredients in this kimchi stew were procured at a local grocery store on Cat Island except the fish, which was freshly caught. "When we started putting it together, something was missing and we went to the large pantry of the hosts who we were staying with," remembers Gilmore. "We found Tiparos fish sauce, which was the ingredient that set off the whole dish. We ended up feeding twenty to thirty local neighbors, and the best part, aside from all the great people there, was having leftovers—however small—to eat the next day." As a shortcut, store-bought kimchi may certainly be used to replace the homemade one described here.

KIMCHI STEW
WITH TUNA AND RAMEN NOODLES

Chef/Owner **JACK GILMORE** | **JACK ALLEN'S KITCHEN** Austin, Texas

KIMCHI

2 pounds napa cabbage

¼ cup sea salt or kosher salt

1 tablespoon grated garlic (from 5 to 6 cloves)

1 tablespoon grated fresh ginger

1 tablespoon sugar

2 to 3 tablespoons fish sauce

1 tablespoon red pepper flakes

8 ounces radish or daikon, peeled and cut into matchsticks

4 scallions, trimmed and cut into 1-inch pieces

MAKES 1 QUART

CUCUMBER RELISH

¼ cup chopped red onion

1 cup peeled, seeded, and chopped cucumber

2 tablespoons chopped fresh cilantro

2 tablespoons rice vinegar

2 tablespoons olive oil

2 tablespoons white sesame seeds

KIMCHI STEW

1 tablespoon toasted sesame oil

2 cups kimchi (homemade or store-bought)

1 tablespoon minced garlic

¼ cup kimchi broth (from jar of kimchi)

1 package instant ramen noodles (soup mix discarded)

6 ounces fresh tuna, chopped

3 scallions, trimmed and cut into 2-inch pieces

Continued

To make the kimchi, quarter the cabbage lengthwise and remove the core. Cut each quarter crosswise into 2-inch-wide strips. Place the cabbage and salt in a large bowl. Using your hands, massage the salt into the cabbage until it starts to soften a bit, then add water to cover the cabbage. Put a plate on top and weigh it down with something heavy, like a jar or can of beans. Let stand for 1 to 2 hours. Rinse the cabbage under cold water three times and let drain in a colander for 15 to 20 minutes. Rinse and dry the bowl used for salting and set it aside to use later.

Combine the garlic, ginger, sugar, and fish sauce in a small bowl and mix to form a smooth paste. Mix in the red pepper flakes.

Gently squeeze any remaining water from the cabbage and return it to the bowl along with the radish, scallions, and seasoning paste. Using your hands, gently work the paste into the vegetables until they are thoroughly coated. (Wearing gloves is highly recommended to protect from stinging, stains, and smells.)

Pack the kimchi into a quart-size jar, pressing down on it until the brine rises to cover the vegetables. Leave at least 1 inch of headspace. Seal the jar with the lid. Let the jar stand at room temperature for 1 to 5 days. You may see bubbles inside the jar and brine may seep out of the lid. Place a bowl or plate under the jar to catch any overflow.

Check the kimchi once a day, pressing down on the vegetables with a clean spoon to keep them submerged under the brine. This also releases gases produced during fermentation. When the kimchi tastes ripe enough for your liking, transfer the jar to the refrigerator. You may eat it right away, but it's best after another week or two.

To make the cucumber relish, combine the onion, cucumber, cilantro, vinegar, olive oil, and sesame seeds in a bowl and mix well. Set aside.

To make the kimchi stew, measure out 2 cups of the homemade kimchi (or substitute store-bought) and chop it into 1-inch pieces. Heat the sesame oil in a medium pot over medium-high heat and stir-fry the kimchi and garlic for 5 minutes. Add 3 cups water and the kimchi broth to the pot, increase the heat to high, and bring to a hard boil. Add the ramen noodles and cook until almost done, about 7 minutes. Add the tuna and scallions to the pot and cook for another 3 minutes. Serve with cucumber relish and additional kimchi sauce, if desired, on top.

SERVES 3 TO 4

"I first encountered the wonderful combination of tomatoes with seafood and ginger in a hot-pot restaurant in Beijing," says Mary Helen Leonard. "Tomato is a popular base for Sichuan hot-pot and Northern Chinese noodle dishes, but is often ignored in American Chinese cuisine. Fish sauce and tomato are both loaded with umami—the fifth flavor—making this light, aromatic soup hearty and satisfying."

CRAB AND ROASTED TOMATO SOUP
IN SPICY GARLIC GINGER BROTH

MARY HELEN LEONARD | culinary instructor, lifestyle writer, and creator of MARYMAKESGOOD.COM

1 cup cherry tomatoes, dressed in olive oil, salt, and pepper

2 tablespoons vegetable oil

4 cloves garlic, minced

1 teaspoon red pepper flakes

1 bunch scallions, sliced and separated into green and white parts

2 tablespoons rice wine (mirin, sake, or Chinese rice wine)

1 (16-ounce) can plain tomato sauce

1 quart chicken stock

1 tablespoon soy sauce

2 teaspoons fish sauce

1 tablespoon grated fresh ginger

1 bunch fresh spinach, chopped

8 ounces lump crabmeat

Salt and freshly ground black pepper

¼ cup chopped fresh cilantro, for garnish

Preheat the oven to 400°F. Spread the cherry tomatoes out over a baking sheet lined with parchment paper. Roast for 15 to 30 minutes, until the tomatoes have shriveled and browned.

Heat a soup pot over medium heat. When the pot is hot, add the vegetable oil, followed by the garlic, red pepper flakes, and the white part of the scallions. Stir-fry for about 5 minutes.

Add the rice wine and deglaze the pan using a wooden spoon. Cook for a few minutes, until the alcohol burns off, then add the tomato sauce, chicken stock, soy sauce, and fish sauce. Bring the mixture to a boil, then lower the heat to maintain a simmer. Cook for about 10 minutes, then add the ginger, spinach, and crabmeat.

Stir until the spinach wilts and the crabmeat is heated through, about 2 minutes. Taste for seasoning, adding more salt, pepper, or red pepper flakes as needed. Garnish with the scallion greens and the cilantro before serving.

SERVES 6

Most people don't realize that fish sauce has roots dating back to ancient Rome, where anchovies were first fermented into *garum*. Today, a potent descendent of *garum* called *colatura di alici*, produced in southwest Italy, can be purchased online or found in gourmet specialty stores. This dish is a play on *spiedini alla Romana*, fried mozzarella cheese bread skewered and served with a garlic anchovy caper sauce. Here, the bread becomes croutons and the anchovy sauce is reinterpreted as a Caesar dressing, with *garum* used in place of anchovy fillets. Kale provides a hearty backdrop to stand up to the bold flavors in the rest of the dish.

KALE CAESAR SALAD
WITH SPIEDINI CROUTONS

VERONICA MEEWES | food journalist at **VERONICAMEEWES.COM**

SPIEDINI CROUTONS

Extra-virgin olive oil, for frying

½ pound fresh mozzarella

8 (⅛-inch) slices ciabatta or high-quality Italian bread

3 large eggs

⅛ cup milk

½ cup all-purpose flour

½ teaspoon sea salt

Freshly ground black pepper

1 cup Italian seasoned bread crumbs

CAESAR DRESSING

2 tablespoons plus ¼ cup extra-virgin olive oil, divided

2 cloves garlic, chopped

1 teaspoon capers, drained

2 egg yolks

Juice of 1 large lemon, plus more as needed

2 teaspoons garum (colatura di alici)

1 teaspoon Dijon mustard

Freshly grated Parmesan cheese

Sea salt and freshly ground black pepper

SALAD

12 ounces kale, tough ribs removed

About ½ cup fresh parsley leaves, torn

Parmesan cheese, for shaving

Continued

To make the spiedini croutons, warm a small amount of olive oil in a sauté pan over low heat. Slice the mozzarella and place an even layer between 2 slices of the bread. The cheese should be about the same width as the bread slices. Repeat until you have 4 sandwiches.

Whisk together the eggs and milk in a dish large enough to fit one of the mozzarella sandwiches. Combine the flour, sea salt, and pepper in another similar-size container. Place the bread crumbs on a flat plate. Dredge the first sandwich in the seasoned flour, coating it thoroughly, followed by the egg mixture. Shake off any excess egg and coat the entire thing in bread crumbs before frying in the olive oil. Once one side is golden brown, 3 to 4 minutes, flip and fry the other side for 3 to 4 minutes. Remove from the pan and set on a paper towel–lined plate to cool. Repeat with the remaining 3 sandwiches.

To make the dressing, heat 2 tablespoons of the olive oil in the same pan used to cook the sandwiches over medium-low heat. Add the garlic and cook until golden, 3 minutes. Add the capers and continue to cook without letting the garlic get too brown. Remove from the heat and let cool. Transfer to a food processor and process until combined.

In a separate bowl, whisk the egg yolks before adding them to the processor, followed by the lemon juice, *garum*, and mustard. Process until creamy and slightly thickened. Very slowly drizzle in the remaining ¼ cup olive oil with the food processor running. The dressing will continue to thicken and emulsify, becoming lighter in color. Season to taste with salt and pepper (and more lemon juice, if desired).

To prepare the salad, chop the kale into bite-size pieces and add the fresh parsley to taste. With gloved hands, massage the Caesar dressing into the kale leaves, working in batches. Use a vegetable peeler to produce curls of Parmesan and lightly toss those with the greens. Divide the salad among six to eight serving plates. Cut the spiedini sandwiches into 1 by 1-inch cubes and distribute those atop the salads before serving.

SERVES 6 TO 8

Chef Edward Kim wanted to create a dish that captured the delight of his first papaya salad enjoyed while studying in New York. "I loved the vegetal crunch, the sweet, sour, and funky tastes," he remembers. "I loved how refreshing it was, and how it had the addictive and masochistic factor of being spicy enough to make me want to satiate the burn in my mouth with more." In this spin-off, he replaced green papaya with kohlrabi for a greener flavor and hardier texture. Candied shrimp is a Korean side he's always loved and wanted to use. "The fish sauce in this recipe adds a nice salty funk to the salad," says Kim. "It gives the salad umami without making it heavy. That's one of the things I love about fish sauce: used in moderation, it adds a smokiness and addictive quality to a dish—similar to MSG, but without leaving you bloated, and without filling your body with overprocessed junk."

CHICKEN AND CANDIED SHRIMP SALAD

Chef/Owner **EDWARD KIM** | **MOTT ST** Chicago, Illinois

CANDIED SHRIMP

2 tablespoons vegetable oil

1 cup dried baby shrimp

1 tablespoon honey

1 tablespoon Korean chili paste (gochujang)

1 teaspoon sesame oil

SALAD

1 cup freshly squeezed lime juice

3 tablespoons sugar

2 tablespoons finely grated jaggery

½ cup fish sauce

4 cloves garlic

6 Thai chiles, finely sliced

½ cup chopped fresh cilantro

½ jalapeño, thinly sliced

1 teaspoon red pepper flakes

2 kohlrabi bulbs, julienned

KAFFIR LEMONGRASS CHICKEN

1 chicken breast

3 cups chicken broth

1 kaffir lime leaf

1 stalk lemongrass

½ shallot, thinly sliced

6 fresh basil leaves, torn, for serving

To make the candied shrimp, warm a sauté pan and add the vegetable oil. Place the dried shrimp in the pan and flip so that the shrimp are evenly coated in the oil. Gently toast the shrimp until it becomes crunchy and develops a nutty flavor, 4 to 5 minutes.

Add the honey and gently toss the shrimp without breaking them up. Add the Korean chili paste and gently toss some more. If the paste is too thick to evenly coat the shrimp, add a small amount of water. Add the sesame oil and toast for about 1 minute more.

The shrimp should be sticky and dried, and should appear candied. Spread them out to dry on a baking sheet—as they cool down, they will become crunchier.

To make the salad, combine the lime juice, sugar, jaggery, fish sauce, garlic, chiles, cilantro, jalapeño, red pepper flakes, and 2 cups water in a large bowl, mixing well so that the sugars dissolve. Add the kohlrabi, cover, and marinate in the refrigerator for at least 3 hours or, better yet, overnight.

Taste the liquid and, depending on how much liquid has leached from the kohlrabi, adjust the flavor: If it is not sweet enough, add a little sugar. If you want it to taste funkier and salty, add a couple more dashes of fish sauce. If you want more heat, add a few more chiles. (Jalapeños will give you bell pepper flavor with added heat; Thai chiles will give you a lip-smacking upfront burn; and red pepper flakes will give you a slow, warm burn.) Set aside.

To prepare the Kaffir lemongrass chicken, place the chicken in the broth with the lime leaf and lemongrass. Bring the broth to a simmer and simmer for 10 minutes. Turn off the heat and cover. The chicken should be cooked through in 20 minutes.

Right before serving, pull the poached chicken into large chunks. Combine the chicken with the salad, and toss together in the marinating liquid. Place the salad on a serving plate and pour a thin layer of the marinating liquid on the bottom of the plate, about ⅛ inch deep. Toss the shallots and basil leaves in the liquid before garnishing. Top the salad with the candied shrimp and serve.

SERVES 4

Though Ryan Pera tends to celebrate Italian cuisine at his Coltivare restaurant, Korean, Thai, and Vietnamese foods are his favorites. He knows all the best Asian restaurants in town, and for the past few years, he's led an Asian culinary tour for the Greater Houston Convention and Visitors Bureau. The inspiration for this dish is a classic Vietnamese duck salad known as *goi vit*, which is traditionally served over banana flowers. Though Pera uses Squid and Three Crabs brand fish sauce at times, he prefers the clean flavor of Red Boat for this recipe.

BRAISED DUCK
WITH GINGER LIME SLAW

Chef/Co-owner **RYAN PERA** | **COLTIVARE** Houston, Texas

GINGER LIME VINAIGRETTE

¼ cup fish sauce

½ cup sugar

¼ cup soy sauce

2 tablespoons chopped scallions

2 tablespoons grated fresh ginger

1 tablespoon minced garlic

2 tablespoons sesame oil

1 cup sunflower oil

BRAISED DUCK

4 duck legs

1 tablespoon kosher salt

4 cloves garlic, smashed

Finely grated zest of 1 orange

1 tablespoon olive oil

1 medium yellow onion, cut into large dice

2 stalks celery, cut into large dice

1 medium carrot, cut into large dice

1 teaspoon whole black peppercorns

2 fresh parsley stems

1 quart chicken stock

1 tablespoon chopped fresh cilantro, plus more for garnish

1 teaspoon fish sauce

1 teaspoon sesame oil

GINGER LIME SLAW

2 cups shredded cabbage

½ cup finely shredded carrots

To make the ginger lime vinaigrette, mix the fish sauce, sugar, soy sauce, scallions, ginger, and garlic together in a bowl. Whisk the oils slowly into the mixture to incorporate. Set aside.

To prepare the braised duck, in a bowl combine the duck, salt, garlic, and orange zest. Mix until the duck legs are evenly coated. Lay the duck legs on a flat tray or plate, meat-side up, and cover with plastic wrap. Place in the fridge and let the meat marinate overnight or for up to 24 hours. Remove the legs and brush off any zest and garlic and set aside.

Preheat the oven to 300°F.

Heat an ovenproof casserole or Dutch oven over medium-high heat. Add the olive oil, then add the duck legs, skin-side down. Sear the legs until golden brown, 2 minutes. Then turn the legs to the meat side and sear until golden brown, 2 minutes more. Remove the legs and set aside.

Place the onion, celery, and carrot in the same pan and cook until lightly browned, 4 minutes. Add the peppercorns, parsley, and stock and bring to a simmer. Add the duck legs and cover the pan. Place in the oven and cook until the duck meat is tender but not falling off the bone, about 2½ hours. Remove the pan from the oven and let the duck legs cool in the liquid. When cool, pick the leg meat off the bones and reserve. Use the liquid for another purpose, such as a soup or gravy.

In a bowl, toss the cooled duck meat with the cilantro, fish sauce, and sesame oil until coated.

To make the ginger lime slaw, in a bowl, mix ½ cup of the ginger lime vinaigrette with the cabbage and carrots and toss to coat. Place the slaw on a serving platter or individual plates. Top with the duck, garnish with cilantro, and serve immediately.

SERVES 2 TO 4

Connie Tran says her favorite dishes are the ones that are simplest, highlighting each ingredient. And while this dish is anything but subtle, each flavor boldly holds its own against the other. "A simple slice of green mango dipped into a sweet and pungent syrup of fish sauce and palm sugar epitomizes the bold flavors of southern Vietnam's 'peasant' food from my childhood," says Tran. "With the addition of sorrel, pecans, and chile, this dish has grown up. Spicy, sweet, sour—the simplicity of this dish lets the ingredients shine."

GREEN MANGO, SORREL, AND CANDIED PECANS
IN SPICY PALM SUGAR SYRUP

Chef/Owner **CONNIE TRAN** | **BEP KITCHEN** Los Angeles, California

Nonstick cooking spray

½ cup whole pecans

4 tablespoons palm sugar (if in disc form, 3 ounces grated), divided

1 tablespoon unsalted butter

1 tablespoon fish sauce

1 whole green mango, peeled and cut into 1-inch cubes (2 cups)

2 to 3 sorrel leaves, coarsely chopped

1 whole red bird or serrano chile, cut crosswise into ⅛-inch slices

Preheat the oven to 350°F. Line a baking sheet with parchment paper and coat with nonstick spray. Coarsely chop the pecans and set aside. Put 1 packed tablespoon of the palm sugar in a small pot. Add the butter and stir over medium-low heat until the butter has melted and the sugar has completely dissolved. Remove the pan from the heat and stir in the pecans. Toss until evenly coated, then spread onto the lined baking sheet and bake for 8 to 10 minutes, until fragrant. Let cool and separate into pieces. Set aside.

For the dressing, put the remaining 3 tablespoons palm sugar into another small pot. Add 1 tablespoon water. Heat over medium-low heat until the sugar has completely dissolved. Remove from the heat and stir in the fish sauce. The mixture should have the consistency of maple syrup.

To assemble the salad, toss the mango, sorrel, and chile in the dressing. Top with the candied pecans and serve chilled.

SERVES 4

MAM NEM
REDIENT : FISH, SALT, WATER
NH PHẦN : CÁ CƠM, MUỐI, NƯỚC

DISTRIBUTOR
IHA BEVERAGE
COMMERCE CA.90040
FL.OZ.(207ML)
T NO
PRODUCT OF VIETNAM

NIM
AN (GRADE A) STEA

T HUONG FISHSAUCE COMPANY

THREE CRABS Brand

SMALL
BITES

Cơm Ăn Liề

SINCE 1908

CKEREL SAU
GOONG BALAY
E DE MAQUE

At Decca in Louisville, Executive Chef Annie Pettry serves caramel corn to her guests as a last bite to signify the end of the meal. "This sweet and spicy caramel corn with fish sauce caramel is one of my favorites because it hits all the bases—sweet, salty, spicy, bitter," she says. "The fish sauce in the caramel adds a deep, savory flavor and provides the salt to the caramel corn. I bet you can't eat just one bite!"

SWEET AND SPICY CARAMEL CORN
WITH CASHEWS AND FISH SAUCE CARAMEL

Executive Chef/Partner **ANNIE PETTRY** | **DECCA** Louisville, Kentucky

16 cups popped corn
(from about ¾ cup kernels)

1 cup cashews, toasted

½ cup (1 stick) unsalted butter

1 cup packed light brown sugar

¼ cup corn syrup

2 kaffir lime leaves

2 tablespoons minced lemongrass

2 teaspoons minced fresh ginger

2 tablespoons fish sauce

½ teaspoon finely grated lime zest

2 teaspoons freshly squeezed lime juice

¼ teaspoon baking soda

1 teaspoon togarashi

Preheat the oven to 200°F. Line two baking sheets with silicone baking mats or parchment paper.

Combine the popped corn and cashews in a large bowl and set aside.

Combine the butter, brown sugar, corn syrup, kaffir lime leaves, lemongrass, and ginger in a tall-sided heavy-bottomed saucepan. Bring to a boil over medium-high heat and simmer for 2 minutes, stirring occasionally. Remove from the heat and whisk in the fish sauce, lime zest, lime juice, and baking soda. Be careful, as the mixture will bubble up.

Quickly and carefully pour the caramel through a fine-mesh strainer onto the popcorn. Stir to evenly coat the popcorn and nuts with the caramel sauce. Sprinkle with *togarashi*.

Spread the caramel corn evenly over the prepared baking sheets. Bake for 45 minutes to 1 hour, stirring every 15 minutes. Remove from the oven and let cool before serving. The popcorn can be stored in an airtight container at room temperature for up to 2 weeks.

MAKES 17 CUPS

At Braise in Milwaukee, Chef David Swanson exclusively sources local produce and meats and often gives them a creative spin using internationally influenced flavors. These crispy pork steam buns are the perfect example. "Using fish sauce in the vinaigrette provides the umami flavor to reinforce the crispy pork on the steamed buns," says Swanson, but he assures that the vinaigrette goes well with any grilled fish or vegetable, as well.

CRISPY PORK STEAM BUNS
WITH FISH SAUCE VINAIGRETTE

Chef/Owner **DAVID SWANSON** |
BRAISE RESTAURANT AND CULINARY SCHOOL Milwaukee, Wisconsin

STEAM BUNS

1 teaspoon active dry yeast

1 cup warm water (110°F)

4¼ cups all-purpose flour, divided

¼ cup granulated sugar

2 teaspoons salt

1 cup hot water (200°F)

3 tablespoons pork fat

CRISPY PORK

½ cup salt

¼ cup packed light brown sugar

3 tablespoons crushed black pepper

3 tablespoons coriander, crushed

1 tablespoon ground cinnamon

1 tablespoon red pepper flakes

4 pounds pork belly

FISH SAUCE VINAIGRETTE

½ cup fish sauce

2 tablespoons rice vinegar

Juice of 1 lime

¼ cup granulated sugar

1 clove garlic, crushed

½ teaspoon chopped dried chiles

½ cup grapeseed oil

To make the steam buns, stir together the yeast and warm water in the bowl of a stand mixer. Then add 3¼ cups of the flour and mix until combined. Let the mixture sit for about 5 minutes to activate the yeast.

Next, mix the granulated sugar and salt with the remaining 1 cup flour in a medium bowl. Add the hot water and then gradually add the pork fat. Add this mixture to the yeast mixture. Mix with the stand mixer's paddle attachment until the dough becomes a smooth, uniform ball. The dough should pull away from the sides of the bowl. Put the dough in a greased bowl and cover with a towel, then let rise until it doubles in size.

To make the crispy pork, mix the salt, brown sugar, black pepper, coriander, cinnamon, and red pepper flakes in a small bowl. Rub the spice mixture all over both sides of the belly. Place in a pan, cover, and set in the refrigerator to cure overnight.

Preheat the oven to 225°F.

Roast the pork belly for 2 hours or until golden brown. Remove from pan, let cool, and cut into ¼-inch dice.

To make the fish sauce vinaigrette, mix the fish sauce, vinegar, lime juice, granulated sugar, garlic, chiles, and ¼ cup water in a small bowl. Slowly whisk in the oil to finish the sauce. Set aside.

To shape the buns, make golf ball–size balls out of the dough, then roll them into 2-inch ovals with a rolling pin and fold in half on the short side of the oval. Let rise again, uncovered, until doubled in size. Steam in a bamboo steamer for 15 minutes. Let the buns cool, then slice and serve with the crispy pork and fish sauce vinaigrette.

MAKES 30 BUNS

While working at Acabar in Los Angeles, chef de cuisine Kevin Luzande realized he'd yet to taste a truly memorable shrimp toast dish anywhere, so when he found himself in the kitchen one day with some extra rock shrimp, he decided to create his own. "I saw this as a great opportunity to experiment with something new and to utilize extra ingredients I had on hand, so I came up with a recipe that I hoped would 'wow' the guest," says Luzande. "It is a slice of country bread with rock shrimp mousse spread on top, deep-fried, and then topped with a sunny-side-up quail egg and *nước chấm* sauce to finish. Everyone loved it and we've kept it on the menu ever since."

SHRIMP TOAST WITH NƯỚC CHẤM

Chef **KEVIN LUZANDE** | Los Angeles, California

SHRIMP TOAST

- 2 gallons canola oil, for frying
- 2 pounds rock shrimp, shelled, deveined, and patted dry with paper towels, divided
- 2 tablespoons minced fresh ginger
- 2 tablespoons minced garlic
- 1 teaspoon freshly ground black pepper
- ½ teaspoon organic cane sugar
- ¾ teaspoon fine sea salt
- 2 teaspoons cornstarch
- 2 scallions, thinly sliced
- 2 egg whites
- 2 pounds fried chicken mix (or karaage mix)
- 1 loaf country white bread, partially frozen for easy slicing
- 1 bunch fresh Thai basil
- 32 quail eggs
- Leaves from ½ bunch fresh cilantro, for garnish

NƯỚC CHẤM

- 2 teaspoons fine sea salt
- 1 cup granulated sugar
- 2 cups filtered water
- 1 cup rice vinegar
- 1 cup freshly squeezed lime juice
- 2½ cups fish sauce
- 2 teaspoons minced garlic
- ¼ teaspoon cayenne pepper
- 1 cup finely shredded carrots
- 2 to 3 scallions, finely sliced
- ½ teaspoon freshly ground black pepper

Continued

To make the shrimp toast, heat the canola oil in a large pot to 250°F.

Coarsely chop 1 pound of the shrimp and put it in a large bowl set over a bowl of ice to keep it cool. In a food processor, combine the ginger, garlic, pepper, cane sugar, salt, cornstarch, and remaining 1 pound shrimp. Purée until smooth, then transfer to the bowl with the chopped shrimp and add the sliced scallions.

In a separate bowl, whip the egg whites until they hold stiff peaks. Gently fold the whipped egg whites into the shrimp mixture.

Put the fried chicken mix in a shallow bowl. Cut the bread into 32 strips (¼-inch-thick slices, 2 by 1¼ inch wide). Lay out the slices of bread on a large cutting board and place a leaf of Thai basil on top of each slice. Using a small offset spatula, spread a 1-ounce spoonful of the shrimp mixture on each slice. Place the shrimp toast into the fried chicken mix, coat thoroughly, and shake off the excess. Carefully place the floured shrimp toast into the hot oil and fry until golden brown, 2 to 3 minutes.

Once the shrimp toast is golden brown, use a slotted spoon to remove it and place onto a paper towel–lined tray to remove excess oil. Cook the remaining shrimp toasts in batches of five at a time.

Cook the quail eggs sunny-side up in a nonstick pan and set aside.

To make the *nước chấm*, place the salt, granulated sugar, and water in a small saucepan and bring to a low simmer. Cook just until the dry ingredients dissolve. Turn off the heat and let the pot sit on a countertop to cool for 30 minutes. Add the vinegar, lime juice, fish sauce, garlic, cayenne, carrots, scallions, and pepper and whisk to combine. Transfer to a bowl for serving.

To serve, place the shrimp toasts on a serving plate, place one quail egg on top of each shrimp toast, garnish with cilantro leaves, and serve with a side of *nước chấm* sauce.

MAKES 32 PIECES

The first time Chef Leah Cohen tested these meatballs at Pig & Khao, she served them as she'd seen them on her travels through Vietnam. "The meatballs were formed around lemongrass stalks, grilled, and put in the sandwich," she says. "I have since changed the way we serve the meatballs at the restaurant since they make great hors d'oeuvres for parties. The fish sauce is the perfect addition as it adds a saltiness and umami flavor." These are equally good served on a baguette as a *bánh mì* or served skewered with Sriracha Mayo on the side.

VIETNAMESE
MEATBALLS

Chef/Owner **LEAH COHEN** | **PIG & KHAO** New York, New York

MEATBALLS

3 tablespoons minced lemongrass

1½ tablespoons cilantro root

2 tablespoons minced garlic

2 tablespoons minced shallot

1 tablespoon salt

1½ tablespoons sugar

¼ cup fish sauce

¼ teaspoons white pepper

1 teaspoon minced kaffir lime leaf

1 pound ground pork

SRIRACHA MAYO

1 cup Kewpie mayonnaise

2 tablespoons Sriracha

3 tablespoons freshly squeezed lime juice

Peanut or canola oil, for frying

To make the meatballs, combine the lemongrass, cilantro, garlic, and shallot in a food processor and process. Mix the lemongrass mixture with the salt, sugar, fish sauce, pepper, kaffir lime leaf, and pork in a bowl. Using your hands, form the mixture into 1-ounce balls.

To make the Sriracha mayo, combine all the ingredients in a bowl and set aside.

Heat the peanut or canola oil in a deep-fryer or on the stovetop in a deep pot to 350°F. Gently add a few meatballs to the oil and cook for approximately 4 minutes, or until cooked throughout. Be careful not to crowd the oil. Remove from the oil with a slotted spoon and set on a paper towel–lined plate to absorb excess oil. Repeat with the remaining meatballs. Serve warm with the Sriracha mayo sauce on the side.

MAKES 12 TO 16 MEATBALLS

After the success of a Hot Joy pop-up at The Monterey, Quealy Watson and Chad Carey turned their concept into a brick-and-mortar restaurant in the spring of 2014 and were quickly named one of the top ten best new restaurants in the country by *Bon Appétit* magazine. These wings have earned a bit of notoriety themselves. "We wanted to take the idea of a fish sauce caramel and combine it with the crunchy textures of Korean fried chicken," says Quealy, "but it needed to be more intense, more funk, more in your face. So we made a caramel with fish sauce, which adds a great depth of umami and an alluring aroma, then went one step further by adding Thai crab paste. The crab paste ups the umami and funk even further, and when combined with the twice-fried wings, you end up with a load of different sensations—funky, sweet, crunchy, addictive little snacks."

CRAB FAT WINGS

Chef/Owner **QUEALY WATSON** | **HOT JOY** San Antonio, Texas

½ cup fish sauce

1½ cups sugar

¼ cup Thai crab (or shrimp) paste in bean oil

6 cups vegetable or peanut oil, for frying

1 cup all-purpose flour

1 teaspoon baking powder

½ cup vodka

1½ cups cornstarch, divided

2 pounds chicken wings, separated into wingettes and drumettes

Kosher salt and freshly ground black pepper

¼ cup roasted salted peanuts, chopped

Cilantro, tender leaves and stems

Bring the fish sauce to a boil in a medium saucepan over medium-high heat and cook until reduced by almost half, about 5 minutes. The fish sauce will darken in color and become very fragrant and pungent. Add the sugar and cook until an instant-read thermometer registers 230°F. The mixture will be thick and dark, like a caramel. Remove from the heat and whisk in the crab paste; set aside and keep warm.

Heat the oil in a large pot fitted with a deep-fry thermometer to 350°F. Meanwhile, whisk the flour, baking powder, vodka, 1 cup of the cornstarch, and 1¾ cups water in a medium bowl. The batter should be very thin, slightly thicker than milk and thinner than cream.

Season the chicken with salt and pepper and toss in the remaining ½ cup cornstarch to coat. Shake off any excess. Working in three batches, coat the chicken with the batter, then fry until the chicken is a light golden brown and crisp, about 5 minutes. A thermometer inserted into the thickest part of the chicken pieces should register 165°F. Immediately toss into the warm caramel, letting the excess drip off. Serve topped with the peanuts and cilantro.

SERVES 4

Chef Jason Dady's latest culinary endeavor, Umai Mi, takes inspiration from Thai, Vietnamese, Chinese, and Japanese cultures, culminating in a fun and boldly flavorful menu. "This dish is inspired by the perfect flavor, umami," says Dady. "The salty, the sweet, the acid, and the fresh vibrant flavors of the herbs bring it all together. I use this sauce in various dishes as it really has the balance that makes your taste buds come alive." Dady recommends using his favorite Red Boat fish sauce in the carrot-papaya slaw.

SHRIMP AND PORK BELLY
BÁNH MÌ

Chef/Owner **JASON DADY** | **UMAI MI** San Antonio, Texas

¼ pound lemongrass

1 pound Florida pink shrimp, peeled and deveined, shells reserved

1 pound braised pork belly

1 green papaya, peeled, seeded, and cut into matchsticks

2 large carrots, cut into matchsticks

½ cup fish sauce

½ cup freshly squeezed lime juice

¼ cup extra-virgin olive oil

¼ cup ginger juice

1 (17.64-ounce) bottle Kewpie mayonnaise

8 mini baguettes

2 English cucumbers, peeled and cut into matchsticks

1 (17-ounce) bottle Sriracha

4 jalapeños, cut into thin rounds

1 small bunch fresh Thai basil

1 small bunch fresh cilantro

1 small bunch fresh mint

In a large stockpot, bring 1 gallon water to a boil. Add the lemongrass and reserved shrimp shells and simmer for 30 minutes over low heat. Strain the shrimp broth through a fine-mesh strainer and return to the pot. Return the broth to a boil, then add the peeled shrimp, cover, and remove from the heat. Let the shrimp poach for 6 minutes, then remove from the broth with a slotted spoon and chill. Discard the broth.

Pan sear the pork belly in a large skillet over medium heat until golden brown. Keep warm for serving in the oven at the lowest setting.

Toss the papaya and carrot with the fish sauce, lime juice, and olive oil in a medium bowl. Set aside. Combine the ginger juice with the mayonnaise in a small bowl and set aside.

To serve, cut the baguettes down the middle lengthwise, but do not cut all the way through. Spread the ginger mayonnaise on both sides inside the baguette. Cut the pork belly into eight ⅓-inch-thick slices and add a slice and 2 or 3 shrimp to each baguette. Layer sliced cucumbers into the sandwich on top of the shrimp and pork belly.

Next, top the cucumbers with a squirt of Sriracha, to taste, a spoonful of the carrot-papaya slaw, and a few jalapeño slices, and all three herbs. Serve immediately.

SERVES 8

Sauce
Phan Thiết

Cơm An Liền

幸福
特別香甜魚露

VEGETABLE
SIDES

quid
BRAND
H SAUCE
AN (GRADE A) STEA

EDIENTS:
tract, Salt, Sugar.

duct contains
(Anchovy)

MAM NEM
INGREDIENT : FISH, SALT, WATER
THÀNH PHẦN : CÁ CƠM, MUỐI, NƯỚC

DISTRIBUTOR
IHA BEVERAGE
COMMERCE CA.90040
NET 7FL.OZ.(207ML)
LOT NO 13.01
PRODUCT OF VIETNAM

Chef Chris Shepherd's first restaurant, Underbelly, pays homage to Houston's cultural diversity, as well as its plethora of local farmers and ranchers. Shepherd is well connected to the city's family-owned Thai and Vietnamese restaurants and has been known to lead tours to his favorite places throughout the Bellaire district. This dish was inspired by chicken wings served with caramelized fish sauce, a popular dish on Southeast Asian menus. Shepherd substitutes the protein for seasonal farmer's market vegetables like okra or broccoli, and it has now become a staple on Underbelly's menu.

CRISPY FARMER'S MARKET VEGETABLES
WITH CARAMELIZED FISH SAUCE

Chef/Owner **CHRIS SHEPHERD** | **UNDERBELLY** Houston, Texas

UNDERBELLY FISH SAUCE

2 tablespoons rice vinegar

¾ cup fish sauce

1½ tablespoons brown sugar

1 clove garlic, peeled

10 sprigs fresh cilantro

MAKES 1 CUP

CRISPY VEGETABLES

Oil, for frying

4 cups seasonal vegetables (such as broccoli or okra), chopped into bite-size pieces if needed

2 tablespoons chopped fresh cilantro

Juice of ½ lime

4 picked cilantro leaves, for garnish

To make the Underbelly fish sauce, in a small saucepan, bring the vinegar, fish sauce, brown sugar, garlic, cilantro, and 1 tablespoon water to a low simmer over medium-low heat for 2 to 3 minutes. Strain through a fine-mesh strainer and set aside.

To make the crispy vegetables, heat the oil (enough to completely submerge the vegetables) in a pot or deep-fryer to 350°F. Carefully drop the vegetables into the oil and fry until tender, but still crispy—30 seconds to a minute. Remove from the oil using a slotted spoon and set on a paper towel–lined tray to drain excess oil. Repeat with the remaining vegetables.

While frying the vegetables in batches, heat a large sauté pan over high heat until the pan is very hot. Pour the Underbelly fish sauce into the pan. It should sizzle and come to an almost instant boil. Cook to reduce the sauce by half.

Place the cooked vegetables into the sauté pan. Toss with the fish sauce and add the lime juice and chopped cilantro. Toss to incorporate. Portion into four bowls or plates and garnish each with a cilantro leaf.

SERVES 4

Pikliz is a Haitian-style pickle dish comprised mostly of cabbage and peppers with a vinegar base. Chef Spencer Bezaire created this Korean kimchi-inspired *pikliz* using *gochujang* and fish sauce. He recommends serving it with fried foods, grilled fish, raw oysters, or even as a zesty snack on its own. "I only use Red Boat fish sauce, for it is the most pure and there are no bitter flavors from additives or artificial fish flavors," he says.

KOREAN
PIKLIZ

Executive Chef/Owner **SPENCER BEZAIRE** | **EL CONDOR**
and Executive Chef/Oyster Director | **L&E OYSTER BAR** Los Angeles, CA

1 head napa cabbage, thinly shredded

1 head red cabbage, thinly shredded

2 large white onions, thinly sliced

3 cloves garlic, chopped

2 large carrots, thinly shredded

1 head cauliflower, cut into in small florets

4 toasted arbol chiles, ground

¼ cup Korean chili paste (gochujang)

2 tablespoons brown sugar

2 tablespoons salt

3 cups white distilled vinegar

½ cup freshly squeezed lime juice

¼ cup fish sauce

Mix the cabbages, onion, garlic, carrots, cauliflower, chiles, chili paste, brown sugar, salt, vinegar, lime juice, and fish sauce and place in a large nonreactive container. Weight the top of it down to submerge all and place in the refrigerator overnight or for up to 1 week, depending on how strong you prefer it to become (less time will yield a milder pickle, while more time makes for a stronger pickle).

MAKES 2 QUARTS

Growing up in a Chinese American household, Michelle Tam never experienced a traditional Thanksgiving dinner. Instead, her family shared an inventive East-meets-West feast by giving traditional Turkey Day sides a cultured twist. "A tangy orange-ginger dressing gives this warm Brussels sprouts slaw a zesty zing that'll liven up your Thanksgiving table," says Tam. And the combination of ginger, fish sauce, rice vinegar, coconut aminos, garlic, and sesame oil gives it an Asian flair that's delicious any time of year (and Paleo!). Coconut aminos, a soy-free seasoning sauce, can be found at your local health food market or online, and the ghee may be replaced with any fat of your choosing (such as coconut oil or bacon drippings).

WARM BRUSSELS SPROUT SLAW
WITH ASIAN CITRUS DRESSING

MICHELLE TAM | food blogger and author of *Nom Nom Paleo: Food for Humans*

SLAW
2¼ pounds Brussels sprouts
3 tablespoons ghee, melted
½ teaspoon kosher salt

DRESSING
1 tablespoon ghee
1 tablespoon minced ginger
1 small shallot, minced (about 1 tablespoon)
2 cloves garlic, minced
⅓ cup freshly squeezed orange juice
3 tablespoons coconut aminos
1½ tablespoons rice vinegar
1 teaspoon fish sauce
1 teaspoon toasted sesame oil

GARNISH
2 scallions, thinly sliced
¼ cup minced fresh cilantro
1½ tablespoons toasted sesame seeds

To make the slaw, preheat the oven to 450°F with the rack in the middle position. Line a baking sheet with aluminum foil. Trim away the stems of the sprouts and remove the outer leaves that come off easily (these can be saved and baked at 350°F to make Brussels sprouts chips).

Slice the sprouts very fine or pass them through the slicing blade of a food processor. In a large bowl, toss the shredded sprouts, melted fat, and salt. Mix well with your hands and spread the shredded sprouts evenly on the prepared baking sheet. Bake for 15 to 20 minutes, flipping and tossing every 5 minutes, until nicely browned and tender.

In the meantime, make the dressing. Melt the ghee over medium heat in a saucepan. Add the ginger, shallot, and garlic and sauté until fragrant, about a minute. Add the orange juice, coconut aminos, rice vinegar, and fish sauce to the saucepan. Bring it to a boil and then lower the heat and simmer the dressing for 5 to 8 minutes, or until it's slightly thickened. Remove the pan from the heat and stir in the sesame oil.

Once the sprouts are done roasting, toss with the sauce, scallions, cilantro, and sesame seeds before serving.

SERVES 8

With two restaurants under his belt and another two on the way, Executive Chef Chris Pandel is known throughout the Chicago area for his rustic, seasonal Italian fare. He discovered *garum*, the ancient Roman fish sauce, while reading about Apicius, the first recorded cookbook author. "Having been a fan of using fish sauce in my cooking for some time, yet cooking mainly a Mediterranean-based menu, I thought *garum* would be an appropriate substitute for the traditional Asian fish sauce," says Pandel. He created his own *garum* for a special collaborative dinner inspired by the food of ancient Rome and continues to bring it out for special occasions.

On a more regular basis, he uses the very similar *colatura di alici*, a fish sauce from Naples, or Red Boat. "Fish sauce finds its way into many items on the menu—broths, vinaigrettes, and especially pasta," he says. "For this raw squash dish, we were looking to really enhance the mid-palate of the dish, as raw squash tends to be sweet and bitter, but then fall off. The fish sauce provided the balance we needed to make the dish successful." He recommends using butternut or Long of Naples squash and either Italian *colatura* or Asian fish sauce.

SHAVED
WINTER SQUASH

Executive Chef/Partner **CHRIS PANDEL** | **BALENA** Chicago, Illinois

SQUASH SALAD

1 pound winter squash, peeled and seeded

1 tablespoon pumpkin seeds, toasted

1 tablespoon sunflower seeds, toasted

1 tablespoon pomegranate seeds

1 red endive, cut into thin 1-inch strips

DRESSING

Juice of 1 lemon

1 teaspoon honey

4 large basil leaves, cut into thin 1-inch strips

1 shallot, minced

2 tablespoons Asian fish sauce or Italian colatura

2 tablespoons grapeseed oil

¼ cup Greek yogurt

Pinch of sugar

Pinch of ground cumin

Pinch of ground coriander

To make the squash salad, use a vegetable peeler to peel shavings off the winter squash. Mix the shavings with the seeds and endive. Set aside.

To make the dressing, place all the dressing ingredients in a bowl and stir together until combined. Toss the squash-seed mixture with a light amount of dressing to start, mashing with your hands to properly combine the salad and integrate the dressing. Continue until the vegetables are evenly coated with dressing. Divide among four plates and serve.

SERVES 4

At Faith & Flower in downtown Los Angeles, Chef Michael Hung complements Southern California's year-long bounty with global influences, a wood-fired oven, and an ever-changing raw bar. Southeast Asian flavors were the inspiration behind this wood oven–roasted summer squash. "The sweet, salty, and sour elements of the palm sugar vinaigrette are rounded out with the umami quality of the fish sauce," says Hung. "It gives the vegetable a funky complexity that adds an interesting dimension of flavor."

WOOD ROASTED SUMMER SQUASH
WITH PALM SUGAR, SOY, AND FISH SAUCE VINAIGRETTE

Executive Chef **MICHAEL HUNG** | **FAITH & FLOWER** Los Angeles, California

ROASTED SQUASH

3 pounds baby green zucchini

3 pounds baby pattypan squash

3 tablespoons blended olive oil

Salt and freshly ground black pepper

VINAIGRETTE

2 medium red onions, finely diced

20 cloves garlic, thinly sliced on a mandoline

1 tablespoon finely diced fresh ginger

2 bay leaves

¼ cup palm sugar, or ½ cup loosely packed light brown sugar

½ cup fish sauce

½ cup soy sauce

1 cup unseasoned rice vinegar

2 cups blended olive oil

Salt and freshly ground black pepper

5 to 6 scallions, very thinly sliced

Korean chili flakes

To make the roasted squash, preheat a wood oven to 600°F (or a regular oven to 500°F). Toss the zucchini and squash in the oil to coat, and season liberally with salt and pepper. Place on an unlined baking sheet and roast for 6 minutes. Remove and cool immediately in the refrigerator to prevent overcooking.

To make the vinaigrette, cook the onions, garlic, ginger, and bay leaves in a sauté pan over medium heat until translucent, about 5 minutes. In a separate pot, combine the palm sugar and 2 tablespoons water over medium heat. Melt the palm sugar and caramelize until golden brown. Add the fish sauce, soy sauce, and rice vinegar. Bring to a simmer and stir to fully incorporate.

Combine the onion-garlic mixture with the vinaigrette base, then add the blended olive oil. Warm the roasted squash in an ovenproof skillet in the oven until hot and slightly blistered. Let cool slightly before adding the vinaigrette. Gently toss well to coat and season to taste with salt and pepper.

Arrange the squash in a bowl and add any residual vinaigrette. Garnish with the sliced scallions and a pinch of Korean chili flakes.

SERVES 6 TO 8 AS A SIDE DISH

The menu changes just about nightly at Restaurant Eugene, where James Beard Award–winning Chef Linton Hopkins selects and combines the best local and global ingredients in honor of his home city of Atlanta. "I love vegetable cookery!" says Hopkins. "Here, greens are elevated to a truly elegant dish with the addition of a simple *gastrique* made with fish sauce and apple cider vinegar. Each of the five basic tastes—sweet, salty, bitter, sour, and umami—come through, resulting in complex layers of flavor." He recommends using any combination of collards, kale, chard, turnip, beet, or mustard greens and an apple cider vinegar that actually smells like fresh apples.

SKILLET GREENS, CRISP SHALLOTS, NƯỚC MẮM APPLE CIDER GASTRIQUE

Chef **LINTON HOPKINS** | **RESTAURANT EUGENE** Atlanta, Georgia

SHALLOTS

2 cups peanut oil

5 shallots, peeled and sliced razor thin across the grain

2 pinches of salt

GASTRIQUE

¼ cup sugar

1 tablespoon red pepper flakes

½ cup high-quality apple cider vinegar

½ cup fish sauce

GREENS

2 pounds mixed winter baby braising greens, cleaned and stemmed

1 tablespoon peanut oil

2 tablespoons bacon grease

Kosher salt and freshly cracked black pepper

To make the shallots, heat the oil to 275°F in a small pot. In small batches, add the shallots and fry until just golden brown, keeping in mind they will continue to darken after being pulled out. Use a slotted spoon to transfer the shallots to a paper towel–lined plate. Top with the salt and set aside.

To make the *gastrique*, melt the sugar in a thick-bottomed pot over medium heat. Add the red pepper flakes and continue to cook until the sugar becomes slightly browned. Add the apple cider vinegar and fish sauce, then stir until well combined. Remove from the heat and reserve. This will keep for months in the refrigerator if stored in an airtight container.

To make the greens, cut them into ½-inch strips. Heat the oil and bacon grease in a large cast-iron skillet over medium-low heat. In batches, add the greens and toss until wilted and glazed with fat, about 1 minute. Season to taste with salt and pepper.

Place the wilted greens on a plate, drizzle with the *gastrique*, and top with the crispy shallots before serving.

SERVES 4

MAM NEM

GREDIENT : FISH, SALT, WATER

NH PHẦN : CÁ CƠM, MUỐI, NƯỚC

DISTRIBUTOR
IHA BEVERAGE
COMMERCE CA.90040

T:7FL.OZ.(207ML)

OT NO 13.013.01

PRODUCT OF VIETNAM

特別香甜魚露

Cơm An Liề

PASTA

KIML

N (GRADE A) STEA

Sauce

Phan Thiết

ET HUONG FISHSAUCE COMPAN

THREE CRABS Bran

During his years as executive chef at Nightwood in Chicago, Chef Jason Vincent became known as the "prince of pork" for winning Cochon 555 in Chicago and the Grand Cochon in Aspen. And now that the *Food & Wine* 2013 Best New Chef has taken a break from the kitchen to plot his next restaurant opening, he's been experimenting with all different realms of cuisine. "The first thing that happened is that I got bit by the 'fermentation bug' really hard," says Vincent. "The other was that I knew absolutely nothing about Asian ingredients and methods and I felt as if I was getting left behind, so I started learning. The fish sauce in this recipe mirrors the flavor of the Parmesan. They're actually very, very similar in flavor." Vincent recommends serving this over a fresh pasta made with cornmeal or with orzo, which turns the dish into more of a stew. Store-bought fish sauce can be substituted, but Jason ferments his own for up to two years.

LATE SUMMER
PASTA SAUCE

Chef **JASON VINCENT** | Chicago, Illinois

FISH SAUCE

15 pounds oily fish carcasses (anchovy, sardines, or mackerel)

Salt, to coat the fish

Ascorbic acid (varies: 1.25 grams of ascorbic acid for every 250 mL of liquid)

PASTA SAUCE

1 small yellow onion, cut into small dice

Spanish olive oil, for sautéing

5 cloves garlic, peeled and very thinly sliced

1 green bell pepper, roasted, skinned, seeded, and finely chopped

1 jalapeño, roasted, skinned, seeded, and finely chopped

1 serrano chile, roasted, skinned, seeded, and finely chopped

2 ripe sauce tomatoes (black plums are ideal), blanched, peeled, and diced

½ cup fresh shell beans, shelled

Salt

TO SERVE

Pasta of your choice

Few drops fish sauce or non-viscous store-bought sauce

Freshly squeezed lemon juice

Spanish olive oil, for drizzling

1 Thai chile, cut into very thin strips

Fresh basil and parsley, for garnish

10 small tomato leaves, for garnish

Parmesan cheese, for garnish

To make the fish sauce, do not rinse or dry the bones. Toss them in the salt and place in a perforated pan, tightly wrapped, with a drip pan underneath. Let stand overnight. The next day, place in clean, sterilized jars with the lids screwed on loosely. The size of the jars does not matter but the bones should be tightly packed into the jars. If you have a small vinegar barrel to do the aging in, that would be ideal. Place at room temperature for at least a year. Check the jars often but do not stir. If you start to see any mold form, throw away the batch immediately.

Separate the liquid in the jars and reserve. Save the bones. In a heavy-bottomed pot with no oil, gently caramelize the bones over low heat, stirring continuously. Once caramelized, cool them completely and recombine with the reserved liquid. Repack in cleaned jars or barrel and let stand for another year. Drain off the liquid in the jar and measure 1.25 grams of ascorbic acid for every 250 mL of liquid. Combine. Freeze overnight in a 1-quart airtight container, then place in a cheesecloth-lined bowl at room temperature until totally melted. Discard any remaining solids. Refrigerate the fish sauce or process in a pressure canner. The fish sauce will last indefinitely as long as the seal stays tight and the jars are refrigerated after opening.

To make the pasta sauce, cook the onion in the olive oil over very low heat, then add the garlic. Next, add the roasted peppers, tomatoes, and shell beans. Stir to combine. Cover with olive oil and cook over a low heat until the beans are tender. Once the beans are cooked, season with salt just to the edge of salty.

Cook the pasta and drain. Using a slotted spoon, scoop the guts of the sauce out of the oil and toss with the pasta. Season to taste with fish sauce and lemon juice. Drizzle with olive oil. Garnish with Thai chile, basil, parsley, tomato leaf, and Parmesan.

MAKES 1 QUART OF SAUCE (8 SERVINGS)

This recipe is Chef Gerard Craft's attempt at re-creating the flavors of the Calabrian delicacy known as *sardella*. The "poor man's caviar," as it's often referred to, is made from baby anchovies and red peppers packed in olive oil, then cured in jars for six or more months before it is spread on bread or eaten with pasta. To mimic the oily, fishy flavor of the *sardella*, Craft actually makes his own fish sauce using Missouri trout, but assures that store-bought Italian *colatura* or Asian fish sauce would serve as a great substitute.

ODE TO SARDELLA

Chef **GERARD CRAFT** | **PASTARIA** St. Louis, Missouri

CHILI PASTE

10 red chiles of moderate heat level, stemmed and seeded

2 cloves garlic

Pinch of salt

Juice of 1 lemon

PASTA AND SAUCE

1 medium yellow onion, cut into ¼-inch pieces

Splash of extra-virgin olive oil

2 anchovy fillets

¼ cup dry white wine

1 (28-ounce) can tomatoes with juices

2 tablespoons Missouri trout fish sauce (or store-bought fish sauce or colatura)

Salt

1 pound fresh spaghetti

2 tablespoons unsalted butter, cold

To make the chili paste, grind all the chiles and garlic with a mortar and pestle until a paste starts to form. Add the salt and lemon juice and continue to work the chiles and garlic until a coarse paste is formed. Transfer to a nonreactive container, cover, and refrigerate for up to 2 weeks. The chili paste may be used right away but is best after the flavors have melded overnight.

To make the pasta and sauce, cook the onion in the olive oil in a large pot over medium-low heat until translucent. Add the anchovies and sauté until fragrant, about 2 minutes. Add ½ cup of the chili paste and continue to cook until very fragrant and the garlic is no longer raw. Add the white wine and cook until almost completely evaporated. Add the tomatoes and cook for 20 minutes, breaking down any large pieces of tomato with a spatula. Add the fish sauce and taste for seasoning. If not using right away, the sauce will keep in the fridge for about a week.

Continued

Bring a large pot of salted water to a boil. Cook the fresh pasta for 3 to 4 minutes, or until the desired level of tenderness. While the pasta is boiling, warm 2 cups of the sauce in a large saucepan or Dutch oven and whisk in the butter until it is well emulsified. Toss the pasta in the sauce with just enough cooking liquid to help glaze. Use tongs to transfer to a serving platter and serve.

SERVES 2 TO 3

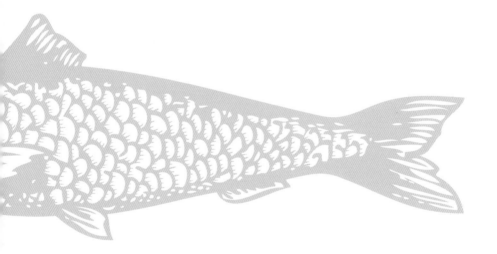

MAM NEM

INGREDIENT : FISH, SALT, WATER
THÀNH PHẦN : CÁ CƠM, MUỐI, NƯỚC

DISTRIBUTOR
IHA BEVERAGE
COMMERCE CA.90040

NET: 7 FL.OZ.(207ML)

LOT NO 13.017.01
PRODUCT OF VIETNAM

MEAT
ENTRÉES

08

SAUCE
(ALAYAN)
QUEREAU

Cơm Ăn Liề

Sauce
Phan Thiết

Though Mei Lin has worked for some of the most revered chefs in the country (such as Wolfgang Puck, Marcus Samuelsson, and Michael Symon), her favorite dishes to cook are sometimes the easiest. "This dish is simply inspired by comfort food," says the winner of *Top Chef* season twelve. "I think it is pretty simple to make at home, and it's most definitely one of my favorite things to eat!" Her fish sauce of choice is Three Crabs brand.

VIETNAMESE
CARAMEL CHICKEN

Sous Chef **MEI LIN** | **INK.** Los Angeles, California

⅓ cup packed brown sugar

½ cup fish sauce

3 tablespoons canola oil

½ medium yellow onion, cut into small dice

2 tablespoons finely diced fresh ginger

2 cloves garlic, minced

1 tablespoon minced lemongrass

8 bone-in, skin-on chicken thighs

¼ teaspoon kosher salt

½ teaspoon freshly ground black pepper

½ teaspoon minced serrano chile

3 scallions, thinly sliced and shocked in ice, for garnish

Jasmine rice, for serving

Heat a large Dutch oven over medium heat and add the brown sugar. Cook until the sugar starts to melt. Decrease the heat to medium-low and cook, swirling the pan frequently, until the caramel is bubbling and turns amber, 4 to 5 minutes. Remove the pan from the heat and very carefully pour in the fish sauce. If the caramel hardens, set the pan over medium-high heat. Stir until the caramel dissolves, then pour it into a heatproof measuring cup or bowl.

Place a skillet over medium-high heat and heat the canola oil. Add the onion and ginger. Cook for 1 minute. Add the garlic and lemongrass and cook for 1 minute. With a slotted spoon, transfer the onion, ginger, and garlic to a bowl.

Add the chicken thighs to the skillet and cook until the chicken no longer looks raw on the outside, about 2 minutes per side. Add the reserved fish sauce caramel, black pepper, and serrano chile. Mix to coat the chicken. Decrease the heat to medium and cook until the chicken is cooked through, turning the chicken every 2 to 3 minutes, about 20 minutes.

Stir in the reserved onions, ginger, lemongrass, and garlic, cook for 2 to 3 minutes, and season with salt. Transfer the chicken and cooked aromatics to a plate. Garnish with the scallions. Serve with jasmine rice.

SERVES 8 TO 10

Chef Andrew Zimmerman has earned a Michelin star for the past four years for his globally influenced, seasonal fare at Chicago's Sepia. Though trained in classic French techniques, he often employs Asian culinary techniques and considers fish sauce one of his most essential kitchen ingredients. For his spice-lacquered duck breasts, he drew inspiration from the fifth-century Apicius text, the first known cookbook. "This collection of Roman recipes was the basic inspiration for the assertive use of spices in the dish, as well as the inclusion of fish sauce in the glaze," says Zimmerman. "The Romans most likely would have used *garum*, but the end result is the same—an underlying savory umami quality that heightens the duck's natural rich flavor."

SPICE-LACQUERED
DUCK BREASTS, BABY TURNIPS, AND TURNIP GREENS

Executive Chef **ANDREW ZIMMERMAN** | **SEPIA** Chicago, Illinois

DUCK GLAZE

½ cup soy sauce

3 tablespoons Thai fish sauce

Finely grated zest and juice of 2 oranges

2 cinnamon sticks

4 whole star anise

4 bay leaves

2 tablespoons honey

1 tablespoon brown sugar

½ Fresno chile, seeded and minced

1 tablespoon crushed coriander seeds

1 tablespoon crushed fennel seeds

Salt

16 baby turnips with tops

4 (7-ounce) boneless duck breasts, fat scored

Freshly ground black pepper

2 tablespoons extra-virgin olive oil

1 clove garlic, crushed

¼ cup chicken stock

2 tablespoons unsalted butter

Continued

To make the duck glaze, combine the soy sauce, fish sauce, orange zest and juice, cinnamon sticks, star anise, bay leaves, honey, brown sugar, and chile in a pot over medium heat. Cook until the liquid has reduced by half. Strain through a fine-mesh sieve, discarding the solids, and add the coriander and fennel seeds. Reserve.

Bring a pot of water to a boil and season it with enough salt to make it taste like the ocean. Have a bowl of ice water nearby, as well.

Remove the greens from the turnips and set aside. Trim the turnips, leaving about ½ inch of the green stem attached. Peel the turnips, keeping them as round as possible. Halve or quarter the turnips, depending on how big they are. Blanch in the boiling water until they are just tender and then shock them in the ice water to stop the cooking. Drain the turnips and dry them on a kitchen towel.

Clean the turnip greens by separating the leaves from the stems. Discard the stems and wash and dry the leaves. Set aside for later.

Preheat the oven to 350°F.

Season the duck breasts with salt and pepper and put them skin-side down in a cold sauté pan. Turn on the heat to medium-high and begin cooking the duck. As the duck skin cooks, it will generate some fat. Pour it off if it starts to come too high up the sides of the duck. Cook the duck breasts for about 7 minutes, until the skin is well browned and crisp. Put the duck, skin-side up, on a rack over a baking sheet and brush on the glaze.

To finish the duck, put the glazed breasts in the oven for about 5 minutes to cook to medium rare (127°F), then allow the duck to rest in a warm place for at least 4 minutes.

Meanwhile, heat the olive oil in a medium sauté pan. Add the garlic and allow it to flavor the oil but do not let the garlic brown. Add the turnip greens and a pinch of salt. Sauté them quickly just to wilt. Add the blanched turnips, chicken stock, and butter. Cook just until the turnips are hot and the stock and butter are glazing the vegetables.

Slice the duck and arrange one breast on each of four plates. Arrange the turnips and greens on the side.

SERVES 4

Chef Todd Duplechan's Austin-based restaurant Lenoir specializes in "warm weather cuisine" from across the globe. This dish is a riff on *larb* salad from Thailand. "When we were looking at *larb*, we noticed how Cajun it was in theory," he explains. "Rice, chiles, fish, herbs, and pork. With that in mind, we took it in that direction by changing the usual ground pork to sour pork sausage, which reminds me of boudin, and adding fried 'softies' (crawfish) to it. The fish sauce vinaigrette is what makes the dish." Duplechan buys his jaggery from a local Indian store, but sugar may be substituted. Bactoferm is a meat starter culture that may be purchased online (www.butcherpacker.com), but store-bought pork sausage can be substituted instead. He also uses a brown jasmine rice from Louisiana called Cajun Grain, but regular jasmine rice will work just as well.

FERMENTED PORK AND RICE SAUSAGE, LARB SALAD, AND FISH SAUCE VINAIGRETTE

Chef/Owner **TODD DUPLECHAN** | **LENOIR** Austin, Texas

FERMENTED PORK SAUSAGE

1 pound cooked rice

½ cup chopped garlic

2 tablespoons kosher salt

1 teaspoon pink salt

3 tablespoons harissa

3½ teaspoons sugar

1 teaspoon Bactoferm, soaked in 1 tablespoon warm water

3½ pounds ground pork

1 pound ground pork fat

1 pound pork sausage casings

TAMAGO

22 large eggs

¼ cup sugar

¼ cup soy sauce

FISH SAUCE VINAIGRETTE

½ (750-mL) bottle Megachef fish sauce

Finely grated zest of 4 limes

Juice of 20 limes

6 Thai chiles, very thinly sliced

¾ cup plus 3 tablespoons jaggery

LARB SALAD

¾ cup raw jasmine rice

20 fried softshell crawfish

Seasoned flour, for dredging

Canola oil, for frying

3 cups Thai basil, picked leaves

1 cup fresh mint marigold

1 cup fresh mint

1 cup fresh cilantro

To make the fermented pork sausage, process the cooked rice, garlic, salts, *harissa,* sugar, and Bactoferm in a food processor. Use gloved hands to mix the rice mixture into the ground pork and pork fat. Transfer to the bowl of a stand mixer fitted with the paddle attachment and beat until blended. Using a sausage stuffer, stuff the mixture into the casings.

After the sausage is stuffed into one continuous coil, place it in a warm (80°F) area of the kitchen to ferment for at least 3 days. There will be a loss of about 25 percent in weight and the color will darken. After the fermentation, smoke the sausage in a smoker to an internal temp of 165°F and then cool. Crumble the cooled sausage into a frying pan and brown over medium-low heat, 5 to 8 minutes.

To make the *tamago*, mix the eggs, sugar, and soy sauce together in a bowl. Then cook like crêpes over medium-low heat in a nonstick pan. Set aside and cool, then cut into ¼-inch ribbons.

To make the fish sauce vinaigrette, whisk together the fish sauce, lime zest, lime juice, chiles, and jaggery until combined. Set aside.

To make the *larb* salad, toast the rice in a sauté pan over medium-low heat, tossing often, until the individual grains are brown. Cool, then coarsely grind in a food processor. Set aside.

Dredge the crawfish in the seasoned flour, then pan-fry over medium heat in the canola oil. Cook for 4 to 5 minutes per side until golden brown. Drain on a plate lined with paper towels.

Toss the basil, mints, and cilantro with the toasted rice, crumbled sausage, and fish sauce vinaigrette. Garnish with the *tamago* and crawfish "softies."

SERVES 10

At West Bridge, Chef Matthew Gaudet showcases his expertise in French cuisine while creatively incorporating local products and international ingredients. "Fish sauce really solidifies the background flavor notes of this dish," says Gaudet. "Grilling the meat with this marinade really creates a depth of flavor reminiscent of some Southeast Asian flavors, but I like to marry those with other elements commonly found around here in New England. To balance the depth of umami there is the brightness of the green tomatoes and brininess of the salad, all being pulled together with fish sauce and the underlying earthy sweetness of the roasted potato purée." He prefers Red Boat brand fish sauce and *kecap manis* or ABC brand sweet soy sauce.

MARINATED GRILLED SHORT RIB
WITH ANCHOVY SALAD, GREEN TOMATO JAM, AND SWEET POTATO PURÉE

Chef/Owner **MATTHEW GAUDET** | **WEST BRIDGE** Cambridge, Massachusetts

SHORT RIBS

4 slices short ribs (½ inch thick across the bone)

Kosher salt and freshly ground black pepper

1½ tablespoons fish sauce

1½ tablespoons Chinese black vinegar

3 tablespoons cabernet vinegar

½ cup sweet soy sauce

2 tablespoons Kentucky bourbon

1 tablespoon minced garlic

1 tablespoon minced fresh ginger

1 teaspoon red pepper flakes

SWEET POTATO PURÉE

2 pounds sweet potatoes

3 tablespoons olive oil

Kosher salt and freshly ground black pepper

GREEN TOMATO JAM

6 green tomatoes

¾ cup sugar

½ cup champagne vinegar

2 tablespoons fish sauce

ANCHOVY SALAD

3 tablespoons olive oil

2½ teaspoons champagne vinegar

1 teaspoon fish sauce

½ cup cracked toasted hazelnuts

8 oil-marinated white anchovy fillets

2 bunches frisée

Picked fresh herbs (parsley, tarragon, chervil, chive)

Continued

To make the short ribs, heat a grill or grill pan until very hot, near smoking. Season the short ribs with salt and pepper. Mix the fish sauce, black vinegar, cabernet vinegar, soy sauce, bourbon, garlic, ginger, and red pepper flakes together to create a marinade. Reserve one-quarter of it for glazing later. Place the ribs in a shallow dish and completely cover both sides with the remaining three-quarters of the marinade, then marinate for at least 30 minutes.

To make the sweet potato purée, preheat the oven to 400°F. Place the sweet potatoes on top of a small amount of kosher salt in a baking dish. Bake until the potatoes are cooked soft; peel while warm; and purée with the olive oil, salt, and pepper.

To make the green tomato jam, in a food processor combine the tomatoes, sugar, vinegar, and fish sauce. Pulse just briefly, but leave the mixture chunky. Transfer to a small pot and simmer over medium heat for 30 to 35 minutes, until it forms a thick jam.

Place the ribs on the grill and brush with the reserved marinade. Turn after 1 minute, brush again, and repeat two more times until they are nicely glazed and medium-rare (about 3 minutes total).

To make the anchovy salad, mix the oil, vinegar, and fish sauce together to make a light vinaigrette. Mix the nuts, anchovies, frisée, and herbs together, then dress with the vinaigrette.

On each plate, spread some sweet potato purée. Place one rib on top and add an equal portion of anchovy salad. Finish with some green tomato jam on the side.

SERVES 4

Chef Evan LeRoy put together a special Asian barbecue menu for a Dinner Lab event and found himself with leftover ingredients. He decided to experiment by adding fish sauce to his pulled pork barbecue sauce at Freedmen's in Austin. "Most Carolina-style pulled pork has a hot sauce–vinegar sauce applied while pulling, but we added fish sauce for an underlying umami kick," he says. "I put together this Carolina-inspired sauce for our pulled pork and it has been a hit with guests ever since." LeRoy recommends serving it piled high on a white sandwich bun, topped with a sharp vinegar coleslaw.

FREEDMEN'S
PULLED PORK

Chef/Pit Master EVAN LEROY | FREEDMEN'S Austin, Texas

PORK

1 (7 to 8-pound) skin off, bone-in pork shoulder

½ cup kosher salt

1 cup coarsely ground black pepper

PORK SAUCE

¼ cup hot sauce (homemade is preferable)

¼ cup fish sauce

½ cup apple cider vinegar

To make the pork, do not trim any fat off the shoulder; it will result in delicious drippings and moisten it throughout the cooking process. Rub the shoulder with the salt and pepper until very well coated on all sides. Shake off any excess rub and smoke in a smoker at 250 to 275°F for 7 hours, or until a crust has formed on the fat cap.

Place the shoulder in the middle of an aluminum foil cross and crimp the foil halfway up the sides of the shoulder. This will allow the top of the shoulder to form a crunchy exterior while keeping the meat moist inside. Continue smoking for 5 hours or until the bone removes easily. Rest for a minimum of 1 hour or until easily handled.

To make the pork sauce, combine the hot sauce, fish sauce, and vinegar in a squeeze bottle and shake to combine.

To finish the pulled pork, remove the bone and pull the pork meat apart with gloved hands. Mix the crunchy exterior parts throughout the pork so there is an even mix of meat, fat, and crust. Season the pork with the pork sauce and mix to combine.

MAKES 5 POUNDS PORK AND 1 CUP SAUCE

Amy Kritzer's blog *What Jew Wanna Eat* is filled with playful interpretations of traditional Jewish dishes, from kimchi quesadilla latkes to Manischewitz ice cream. Kritzer says brisket is one of her favorite cuts of meat to play with, and she's braised it in everything from wine to whiskey, coffee to beer. This version is filled with tang and sweetness thanks to the addition of ginger, brown sugar, mustard, and fish sauce. These enhance the brightness of the other ingredients and add depth. "Throw it in a pot with a bunch of other ingredients and just let go, and you can transform the tough meat into a tender, cut-with-a-spoon delicacy," she says. "Serve as tacos, over mashed potatoes, or just straight from the pot for an easy but impressive meal!"

MUSTARD AND BEER-BRAISED
BRISKET

AMY KRITZER | recipe developer and creator of **WHATJEWWANNAEAT.COM**

1 (4-pound) flat-cut brisket, trimmed to leave ½ inch fat

1 tablespoon kosher salt

2 teaspoons freshly ground black pepper

2 tablespoons Dijon mustard

2 tablespoons grapeseed oil or another high smoke point oil (such as canola)

2 large yellow onions, thinly sliced

4 cloves garlic, smashed

1 tablespoon minced fresh ginger

¼ cup all-purpose flour

3 cups beer, such as bock

½ cup packed light brown sugar

2 tablespoons fish sauce

¼ cup white wine vinegar

1 cup beef stock (preferably homemade)

Fresh cilantro, for garnish

Bring the brisket to room temperature for 30 minutes, then season liberally on both sides with the salt, pepper, and mustard. Heat the grapeseed oil in a large, heavy-bottomed pot or Dutch oven over high heat. Carefully place the brisket, fat-side down, in the pan. Brown without moving for 5 minutes. Then turn over and brown for 3 minutes more. The outside of the meat should be golden brown.

Remove the brisket and transfer to a plate. Decrease the heat to medium and add the onions. Sauté while stirring with a wooden spoon until the onions are golden brown and wilted, 5 to 7 minutes. Then add the garlic and ginger and sauté for 1 minute more while stirring. Add the flour and sauté until the flour smells a bit nutty, 3 to 5 minutes.

Add the beer to deglaze, scraping the bottom of the pan with the wooden spoon. Scrap up any onions stuck to the bottom. Add the brown sugar, fish sauce, white wine vinegar, and beef stock and bring to a simmer over medium heat. Put the brisket back in, lower the heat to medium-low, and cover. Make sure the brisket is not entirely submerged in the liquid. Simmer for 4 hours, or until the brisket is very tender but not falling apart.

When the brisket is ready, let the meat cool in the sauce and refrigerate overnight to let the flavors meld. The next day, skim the fat off the top of the sauce (leaving about ¼ inch of fat for flavor). Reheat the brisket in the sauce on the stovetop over medium heat. Then remove the brisket and cook the sauce over medium-high heat until it thickens slightly and has reduced by one-quarter, about 5 minutes. The sauce will thicken more as it continues to cool.

Slice the brisket against the grain and serve with the onion sauce and cilantro.

SERVES 6 TO 8

Kim and Hong Pham, the food bloggers behind The RavenousCouple.com, were both raised in first-generation immigrant Vietnamese American families. *Thit kho*, caramelized braised pork belly and eggs, was one of their staple dishes while growing up. In order to get an extra-flavorful, golden brown caramelization on the pork belly, they suggest using young coconut juice, though canned coconut juice will also work in a pinch. "The pork belly of the *thit kho* is so succulent and rich, we confess we sometimes only nibble at the fatty portion or eat half," says Kim. "But to help cut down on the richness and fattiness, our favorite way to eat this is with *dua gia* (pickled bean sprouts, chives, carrots, and onions). It adds a great crunch and just the right amount of acidic tartness to the sweet and savory melt-in-your-mouth pork belly." For more complex sauce, they suggest adding five spice, star anise, fennel, coriander seeds, or cinnamon in a stainless-steel tea strainer while the dish braises.

THIT KHO CARAMELIZED
BRAISED PORK BELLY AND EGGS

KIM AND HONG PHAM | creators of **THERAVENOUSCOUPLE.COM**

DUA GIA
(PICKLED BEAN SPROUTS)

1 pound bean sprouts

2 carrots, finely shredded

1 bunch chives, cut in
    2 to 3-inch segments

1 medium red onion, thinly
    sliced

Distilled white vinegar

Salt

Sugar

PORK BELLY AND EGGS

2 pounds pork belly, cut in
    2 to 3-inch pieces

Juice of 2 young coconuts,
    or 4 cups canned coconut
    juice

4 hard-boiled eggs, peeled

¼ cup fish sauce

1 to 2 shallots, thinly sliced

2 to 3 cloves garlic, gently
    crushed

Freshly cracked black pepper

Steamed rice, for serving

Continued

To make the pickled bean sprouts, combine the sprouts, carrots, chives, and onion in a plastic container with a lid. Add a mixture of 1 part vinegar to 3 parts water to cover. Season with a bit of salt and sugar to cut down on the acidity. Close the container and set in the refrigerator. The pickled vegetables should be ready after 1 day and last for about 1 week.

To make the pork belly and eggs, parboil the pork belly in boiling water in a large pot for 3 to 4 minutes. Dump out the water and rinse off the pork and the pot. Return the pork to the pot and add the coconut juice.

Add the eggs, fish sauce, shallots, and garlic. The liquid should be generous enough to cover both the pork and eggs, guaranteeing even caramelization. If needed, add a bit of water or additional coconut water. Bring to a rolling simmer over medium-high heat, cover with a lid, and decrease the heat to low. Braise for at least 1 hour or up to 2½ hours. The natural sugars of the coconut juice and fish sauce will caramelize the pork and eggs.

Taste the sauce and adjust with additional fish sauce or sugar. Add plenty of cracked pepper just before serving with fresh steaming hot rice. Top with the pickled bean sprouts.

SERVES 4 TO 6

QUID
BRAND
SH SAUCE

GREDIENTS:
Extract, Salt, Sugar.

roduct contains
sh (Anchovy)

特別香甜魚露

SEAFOOD
ENTRÉES

Cơm Ăn Liề

Sauce
Phan Thiết

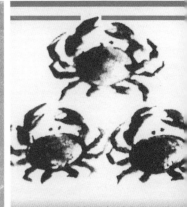

ET HUONG FISHSAUCE COMPAN

THREE CRABS Bran

Chef duo Vinny Dotolo and Jon Shook draw inspiration from the many cultures within the greater Los Angeles area for their restaurants animal and Son of a Gun. The *Hamachi* Tostada on the menu at animal combines Japanese, Latin, and Vietnamese flavor in one dish. The accompanying fish sauce vinaigrette can also be used on pork, beef, chicken, and fish, though Dotolo and Shook recommend using it with vegetables, explaining, "The vinaigrette has the ability to add a lots of depth and liven up a dish without adding too many ingredients."

HAMACHI TOSTADA
WITH FISH SAUCE VINAIGRETTE

Chefs/Co-owners **VINNY DOTOLO & JON SHOOK** | **ANIMAL** Los Angeles, California

CRISPY SHALLOTS

1 quart peanut oil

1 cup shallots, cut into ¼-inch wheels

½ cup all-purpose flour

Kosher salt

TOSTADAS

4 corn tortillas

Kosher salt

AVOCADO MASH

1 Hass avocado, pitted and peeled

2 teaspoons freshly squeezed lemon juice

½ teaspoon kosher salt

SLAW

½ head green cabbage, cored and cut into ⅛-inch-thick strips

1 serrano chile, cut into ⅛-inch rounds

½ medium red onion, cut into ⅛-inch-thick half-moons

4 scallions, sliced on an angle

¼ cup peanuts, toasted

½ cup fresh cilantro leaves

½ cup fresh mint leaves

¼ cup fresh opal basil leaves

¼ cup fresh Thai basil leaves

2 teaspoons kosher salt

FISH SAUCE VINAIGRETTE

½ tablespoon Microplaned garlic

¼ cup finely diced shallot

2 tablespoons Microplaned fresh ginger

8 teaspoons finely grated lemon zest

2 tablespoons freshly squeezed lemon juice, strained

¼ cup plus 2 teaspoons sugar

6 tablespoons fish sauce

1 cup rice wine vinegar

8 ounces hamachi, sliced into ⅛-inch pieces

Kosher salt

Continued

To make the crispy shallots, heat the oil in a saucepan over medium-low heat. In a large bowl, stir the shallots with the flour to lightly coat. Shake to remove any excess flour. Once the oil has reached 250°F, fry the shallots until golden brown, about 1 minute. Remove using a slotted spoon and drain on a plate lined with paper towels. Season lightly with salt to taste. When you have fried all the shallots, increase the oil temperature to 325°F.

To make the tostadas, fry the tortillas (one at a time) in the oil you used for the crispy shallots until light golden brown, 1 minute. Remove using a slotted spoon and drain on a plate lined with paper towels. Season lightly with salt.

To make the avocado mash, combine the avocado, lemon juice, and salt in a bowl. Mash with a whisk, but leave small chunks.

To make the slaw, combine the cabbage, chile, onion, scallions, peanuts, cilantro, mint, basils, and salt in a large bowl. Mix until fully incorporated and set aside.

To make the vinaigrette, combine the garlic, shallot, ginger, lemon zest, lemon juice, sugar, fish sauce, and vinegar in a bowl. Stir until fully incorporated. Add ½ cup of the fish sauce vinaigrette to the slaw mixture. Gently toss until fully incorporated. Let stand for 2 minutes to marinate.

To assemble the tostadas, spread 1 tablespoon of avocado mash on each tortilla. Thinly layer the *hamachi* slices on top of the avocado mash and season the *hamachi* with salt. Add the slaw on top to form a dome shape on top of the fish. Add crispy shallots on top of the dome. Repeat with the remaining three tortillas and serve.

SERVES 4

After three consecutive James Beard Foundation Award nominations for Best Chef: Northeast and three Cochon 555 wins, Chef Matt Jennings decided to close his Providence bistro to open a new restaurant in his home city of Boston. Townsman pays homage to his New England roots by showcasing the region's best ingredients, with dishes such as this. "It's a perfect summer dish—light, yet savory and flavorful," says Jennings. "I attempt to balance the flavors with subtle sweetness from the peaches, the shrimp, and a light marinade—almost a dressing—with the juices from the peach and a drizzle of flavorful fish sauce. The fish sauce helps ground the dish and lets the fresh seafood shine."

GRILLED PEACHES, CRISPY MAINE SHRIMP, CHILES, AND HERBS

Chef/Owner **MATT JENNINGS** | **TOWNSMAN** Boston, Massachusetts

½ cup (1 stick) unsalted butter, at room temperature

1 teaspoon rice vinegar

1 tablespoon brown sugar

2 tablespoons fish sauce, plus more for seasoning

1 teaspoon kosher salt

4 ripe peaches, halved and pitted

Canola oil

8 whole Maine shrimp, head-on and shell-on (U10 preferred)

Cracked white pepper

1 teaspoon Korean chili flakes, plus more for seasoning

GARNISH

Fresh mint leaves

Fresh thyme leaves

Fresh Thai basil leaves

Fresh chervil leaves

In a small bowl, stir the butter until smooth. Add the rice vinegar, brown sugar, fish sauce, and salt and mix until combined. Set aside.

Heat a grill to high. Brush the peaches with canola oil and grill until golden brown and just cooked through, but marked well, 4 to 5 minutes. Set aside in a warm place.

While the peaches are coming to room temperature, cook the shrimp. Gently coat the shrimp with just a tablespoon of canola oil, season well with salt and white pepper, and sprinkle with the Korean chili flakes. Place on the hot grill. The shrimp will only take about 2 minutes per side to cook and, because they are so tender, even the shells can be eaten when they come off the grill. When they are done, they should be gently charred, well marked and cooked through. Slice the peaches, add the shrimp to the bowl, and toss with the liquid from the grilled peaches and the brown sugar–fish sauce blend. Finish with another pinch of Korean chili flakes and fish sauce to taste. Garnish with fresh herbs and serve.

SERVES 4

With this dish, Hakkasan's executive chef Ho Chee Boon shows that some of the most delicious dishes stem from tradition and are best left uncomplicated. He uses a very traditional Cantonese method to steam the fish, then slices and serves it with fresh bamboo shoots and fried radishes. "The recipe is very simple so you can really taste the freshness and actual flavor of the fish," says Boon. "Dover sole is unique and delicate in flavor, and the fish sauce really draws that out." Boon stresses the importance of using the freshest available ingredients and, though the Hakkasan team makes their own fish sauce from scratch, Boon recommends purchasing an Asian fish sauce to save time. Yellow rock sugar, often called blooming lump candy, can be purchased online or found in Asian markets.

STEAMED DOVER SOLE
WITH FRIED CHOPPED RADISH IN SOYA SAUCE

Executive Chef **HO CHEE BOON** | **HAKKASAN** Las Vegas, Nevada

SOYA SAUCE

2 tablespoons soy sauce

2 tablespoons fish sauce

1 teaspoon Xiao Xing cooking wine

2 teaspoons yellow rock sugar (10 grams)

2 small strands cilantro

FISH

2 (6-ounce) pieces live Dover sole

⅔ cup coarsely chopped napa cabbage

Salt

⅔ cup fresh bamboo shoots, peeled and cut into thin slices

⅓ cup sliced radish

¼ cup canola oil

2 teaspoons finely chopped scallion

To make the soya sauce, bring a pot of water large enough to set a bowl over for steaming to a boil. Combine the soy sauce, fish sauce, cooking wine, rock sugar, and 2½ tablespoons water in a bowl. Add the whole strands of cilantro. Cover and steam over high heat for 5 minutes, or until the rock sugar has dissolved. Set aside.

To make the fish, fillet and skin the Dover sole. Cut it into thick slices and set aside for later. Lightly stir-fry the cabbage with some salt.

Place the cabbage on a plate. Next, place the Dover sole slices and bamboo shoot slices on top of the cabbage, with the bamboo shoots resting between each slice of sole. Place the plate in a bamboo basket and steam the dish for 5 minutes and 20 seconds, making sure there is plenty of water in the pot. Remove the dish from the steamer and carefully pour away any extra water.

Heat the oil in a small sauté pan over medium heat. Fry the radish until crispy, 1 minute. Place the fried radish on top of the fish, followed by the sauce, and garnish with the scallion. Serve immediately.

SERVES 2

A traditional Thai condiment, *nam phrik pla* is typically composed of fish sauce and thinly sliced red and green chiles. At Sway in Austin, Executive Chef Alexis Chong puts her own spin on the Thai classic, introducing grated garlic, shallots, and pineapple to round out the flavors and add body to the sauce. The sauce is then used to complement blue crab fried rice, a menu item that features egg, lemongrass, scallion, and Thai basil. She recommends starting with Megachef fish sauce, a brand available in many Asian grocery stores. Since the heat of Thai chiles varies greatly with the seasons, Chong recommends using anywhere from twelve to twenty, depending on spice preference.

BLUE CRAB FRIED RICE
WITH NAM PHRIK PLA

Executive Chef ALEXIS CHONG | SWAY Austin, Texas

NAM PHRIK PLA

- 1 clove garlic, peeled and Microplaned
- 1 medium shallot, peeled and Microplaned
- Small piece of pineapple, peeled and Microplaned
- ¼ cup fish sauce
- 12 to 20 red and green Thai chiles (depending on heat), thinly sliced
- 8 fresh cilantro stems, thinly sliced

FRIED RICE

- 2 tablespoons thinly sliced ground lemongrass, tender white part only
- 4 tablespoons oil (canola or peanut), for sautéing, divided
- 2 tablespoons minced garlic
- 2 tablespoons minced fresh ginger
- 2 tablespoons shallots, peeled and thinly sliced on a mandoline
- 2 tablespoons thinly sliced scallion (both green and white parts)
- 3 large eggs
- 1½ cups jasmine rice, cooked and cooled overnight
- 3 tablespoons lump blue crabmeat
- 3 tablespoons white soy sauce (shoyu)
- 3 tablespoons fish sauce
- Salt and freshly ground black pepper (optional)

GARNISH

- Crispy shallots
- ½ cup mixed fresh Thai basil and cilantro

To make the *nam phrik pla,* combine the garlic, shallot, pineapple, fish sauce, Thai chiles, and cilantro stems in a small bowl and stir until blended. Set aside.

To make the fried rice, in a very hot wok, heat 2 tablespoons of the canola oil and sauté the garlic, ginger, shallots, and lemongrass until light golden brown, about 90 seconds if the wok is hot enough. Add the scallion and eggs.

When the eggs are halfway done cooking sunny-side up, pour the remaining 2 tablespoons oil into the center of the pan and add the cooled, cooked rice. Stir-fry until the eggs are cooked through and the rice is mixed well with the other ingredients. Add the crabmeat and toss gently to heat through, taking care not to break up the crab too much. Rehydrate the rice by adding the soy sauce and fish sauce. Taste, adding salt and pepper if desired.

Top the crab fried rice with crispy shallots and fresh herbs, then serve accompanied with the *nam phrik pla.* The sauce is very strong in heat and salinity so the serving size will vary with personal preference.

MAKES A LARGE PORTION FOR 1 OR A SIDE DISH FOR 3

Since opening State Bird Provisions in 2011, Chef Stuart Brioza and his wife, pastry chef Nicole Krasinski, have been earning well-deserved accolades each year—including a Michelin star for the past two. Many of their imaginative and carefully crafted dishes are served from dim sum carts. Larger dishes can be ordered off the menu, such as this trout, which has become one of Brioza's signature items. "The Red Boat fish sauce adds an indescribable underlay of flavor and umami to a traditional brown butter–citrus sauce in this dish," describes Brioza. "I love that it gets people wondering where all the flavor is coming from."

RICE-SEARED RED TROUT
WITH MANDARIN AND HAZELNUT BROWN BUTTER

Chef/Co-owner **STUART BRIOZA** | **STATE BIRD PROVISIONS** San Francisco, California

SAUCE

2½ tablespoons fish sauce

2½ tablespoons freshly squeezed lime juice

1 teaspoon finely grated fresh ginger

½ teaspoon finely grated garlic

½ cup (1 stick) unsalted butter

2 tablespoons fresh ginger, cut into matchsticks

TROUT

1 cup jasmine rice

4 (3-ounce) skin-on portions trout

Salt and freshly ground black pepper

¼ cup olive oil

1 mandarin, segmented

12 fresh mint leaves

12 fresh cilantro leaves

¼ cup hazelnuts, toasted and cracked into small pieces

To make the sauce, combine the fish sauce, lime juice, grated ginger, garlic, and 2½ tablespoons water and mix well. In a small saucepan, brown the butter, starting from a cold pan, over medium heat. Once brown, remove the pan from the heat and add the cut ginger. After about 10 seconds, add the fish sauce–lime juice mixture and quickly simmer to lightly emulsify. Set aside.

To make the trout, purée the raw jasmine rice in a blender until it becomes a powder, then toast the powder over low heat in a dry sauté pan until lightly brown. Season the fish with salt and pepper, then coat with the toasted rice powder on the skin side.

Heat a cast-iron pan over medium-low heat. When hot, add the olive oil to coat the pan and look for little wisps of smoke to tell if it is hot enough to sear. Gently add the fish, skin/rice-side down, pressing until the fish skin flattens out. Add the remaining portions in the same manner. Cook the fish 70 percent on the skin side, about medium-rare, and flip over in the pan for about 10 seconds before removing from the pan to a warm plate.

Immediately spoon the finished sauce over the trout, followed by the mandarins, mint, cilantro, and toasted hazelnuts. Serve immediately.

SERVES 4

Celebrity chef and *Bizarre Foods* host Andrew Zimmern fondly remembers the first time Chef Ed Lee prepared him frog legs cooked in fish sauce at 610 Magnolia in Louisville. Zimmern has since re-created the dish countless times—until he found himself without frog legs one day and realized halibut was a delicious substitution, made even better by the addition of a smoky barrel-aged fish sauce. "The aged sauce pulls all the nut and toast flavors from the butter, accents all the grassy nose of the celery, plays Abbot to the lemony Costello, coaxes the briny ocean from the flat fish," describes Zimmern. "It doesn't seek to dominate. It's the oldest play in the book. The good soldier." BLiS barrel-aged fish sauce can be purchased online or found in specialty stores, but if it is unattainable, Zimmern recommends using Red Boat's conventional fish sauce. The final dish is best served with rice and miso-glazed eggplant.

HALIBUT
WITH BROWNED BUTTER, LEMON, AND AGED FISH SAUCE

Celebrity Chef **ANDREW ZIMMERN** | Minneapolis, Minnesota

¼ cup wheat berries

½ cup (1 stick) salted butter

3 tablespoons grapeseed or canola oil

4 (6-ounce) skinless halibut fillets

Kosher salt and freshly ground black pepper

3 celery stalks, thinly sliced

1 bunch scallions, minced (1 cup)

1 dried hot chile, such as arbol

2 tablespoons freshly squeezed lime juice

3 tablespoons BLiS barrel-aged fish sauce

Steamed white rice, for serving

Miso-glazed eggplant, for serving

In a small saucepan of boiling water, cook the wheat berries until tender, 20 to 40 minutes. Drain and spread out on a plate to cool. In a small skillet, toast the wheat berries over medium-high heat until golden and crunchy, 7 to 8 minutes. Meanwhile, in a small saucepan, melt the butter. Cook over medium heat until golden brown and nutty-smelling, 5 to 7 minutes. Set aside.

In a large nonstick skillet, heat the oil until shimmering. Season the halibut with salt and pepper and cook over medium-high heat until browned on both sides and just cooked through, 3 to 4 minutes per side. Transfer to a plate. Add the celery, scallions, and dried chile to the skillet and cook, stirring, for 1 minute. Add the brown butter, lime juice, and fish sauce and cook until the sauce is slightly thickened, about 2 minutes. Add the fish and turn to coat in the sauce. Discard the dried chile.

Transfer the fish and sauce to a platter and garnish with some of the toasted wheat berries. Serve with rice and miso-glazed eggplant.

SERVES 4

Before opening The Federal Food, Drinks & Provisions in Miami, Chef Cesar Zapata gained a cult following for Phuc Yea!, his three-month long south Vietnamese pop-up restaurant in a graffiti and hip-hop shop. This dish quickly became a signature item, and he'll be relaunching it once the brick-and-mortar location opens. "We chose to feature rock lobster because it's a local ingredient that is highly seasonal and naturally sweet," describes Zapata. "The fish sauce gives it a caramel and salty, umami quality that neither soy sauce nor salt can achieve, making it a delicious counterpoint for the sweet lobster."

LOBSTER
WITH FISH SAUCE CARAMEL

Chef/Owner **CESAR ZAPATA** | **THE FEDERAL FOOD, DRINKS & PROVISIONS** Miami, Florida

FISH SAUCE CARAMEL

1 pound white, brown, or palm sugar

2 tablespoons freshly squeezed lemon juice

1¼ cups fish sauce

½ cup sweet chili sauce

¼ cup sliced fresh jalapeños

1 ounce ginger, cut into matchsticks

1 bunch scallions, sliced (white and green parts)

LOBSTER

2 whole spiny lobsters

Salt and freshly ground black pepper

2 tablespoons canola oil

¼ cup light beer

½ cup (1 stick) unsalted butter, cut into small pieces

To make the fish sauce caramel, heat ¾ cup water, the sugar, and the lemon juice in a heavy saucepan over medium heat. Let the sugar boil until it turns a dark caramel color. Remove the saucepan from the heat before the sugar reaches the color of coffee. As soon as it's removed from the heat, add the fish sauce and stir or whisk until the bubbling settles down and the sauce is smooth. Add the chili sauce, jalapeños, ginger, and scallions. Set the sauce aside and let it cool.

To make the lobster, with a chef's knife, butterfly the lobster tail by slicing it in half the long way. Be careful not to cut all the way through to the shell. You can also ask the fishmonger to butterfly the lobster tails for you.

Season the lobsters with salt and pepper. Heat the oil in a large sauté pan over medium-high heat. Place the lobsters flesh-side down and sear them until golden brown on that side, 2 to 3 minutes. Once the lobsters are browned, add ¼ cup of the fish sauce caramel, the beer, and cover. Cook for 5 to 6 minutes, then uncover. Let the sauce reduce until it reaches a syrup consistency, 2 to 3 minutes. Remove the lobsters and place them on a serving plate. Whisk the butter into the sauce to emulsify. Pour over the lobsters and serve immediately.

SERVES 2

The James Beard Award–winning chef Michelle Bernstein (Best Chef: South 2008) has been dazzling diners for more than a decade with dynamic Latin-Caribbean cuisine inspired by her travels, as well as her upbringing by an Argentine-Jewish mother and Italian-Jewish father. "The inspiration for this recipe comes from a sauce I tasted in Belize over ten years ago and adapted into my own," says Bernstein, noting that the original was much spicier. "With the creaminess of the coconut, spiciness of the chile, and fragrance of the ginger and lemongrass, nothing rounds out the perfect flavor and covers every possible angle of the palate like the fish sauce."

MUSSELS
IN COCONUT CHILI BROTH

Chef/Owner **MICHELLE BERNSTEIN | SEAGRAPE** Miami, Florida

1 teaspoon minced lemongrass, tender white part only

1½ shallots, chopped

1 clove garlic, chopped

½ tablespoon finely chopped fresh ginger

1 cup unsweetened coconut milk

1 (1-inch) piece jalapeño with seeds, chopped

¼ cup chopped fresh cilantro

1½ tablespoons nước mắm (Vietnamese or Thai fish sauce)

1 cup chicken stock

3 to 5 tablespoons unsalted butter

5 dozen mussels

Crispy shoestring potatoes, for serving

Place the lemongrass, shallots, garlic, ginger, coconut milk, jalapeño, cilantro, *nước mắm*, stock, and butter in a blender and purée until smooth.

Place 1 to 2 dozen mussels in a large sauté pan with a tight-fitting lid (the amount will depend on the size of the pan) and add enough sauce to cover half the mussels. Cover and heat over medium heat for 2 to 3 minutes or just until the mussels start to open. After 3 minutes, remove any mussels that have not opened and discard. Swirl 1 tablespoon of the butter into the pan of mussels. Transfer the mussels and sauce into a large bowl and repeat with the remaining mussels and butter until all the mussels have been cooked.

Serve with crispy shoestring potatoes.

SERVES 4 TO 6

At Korean-Southern fusion diner Sobban and Heirloom Market BBQ in Atlanta, Chef Jiyeon Lee and her husband, chef and co-owner Cody Taylor, celebrate the cuisine of their contrasting backgrounds by marrying the flavors of her South Korea and his American South. "Fish sauce is a tough ingredient to incorporate into Western cuisine," admits Lee. "Koreans use it for making kimchi mainly. Some regions season savory egg custard with fish sauce or brine baby shrimp. This dish is similar to a Korean egg custard dish we call *gaelan-jjim*." Lee prefers the Three Crabs brand fish sauce and, as a variation, recommends adding red bell pepper or Thai chiles to the frittata before cooking.

ZUCCHINI TOFU SHRIMP FRITTATA
WITH FISH SAUCE

Chef/Co-owner **JIYEON LEE** | **SOBBAN** Atlanta, Georgia

8 large eggs

¼ cup heavy cream

½ cup zucchini, cut into matchsticks

¾ cup firm tofu, crumbled

5 ounces medium shrimp (21 to 25 count)

5 tablespoons chopped scallions

¼ cup fish sauce

¼ teaspoon freshly ground black pepper

Vegetable oil

Sprouts (optional)

Preheat the oven to 375°F.

Beat the eggs in a medium bowl, then add the heavy cream and mix well. Add the zucchini, tofu, shrimp, scallions, fish sauce, and pepper and mix thoroughly. Lightly oil a cast-iron pan or thick ovenproof skillet and heat the pan on the stove until hot. Pour the egg mixture into the pan, then transfer to the oven for 17 to 20 minutes. Insert a wood skewer all the way to bottom to check for doneness. The frittata is done when the skewer is removed cleanly.

Remove and let cool a bit before cutting. Garnish with sprouts, if using, and serve.

SERVES 6 TO 8

QUID BRAND H SAUCE

EDIENTS:
tract, Salt, Sugar.
duct contains
Anchovy)

Cơm An Liề

MAM NEM
INGREDIENT : FISH, SALT, WATER
THÀNH PHẦN : CÁ CƠM, MUỐI, NƯỚC

DISTRIBUTOR
IHA BEVERAGE
COMMERCE CA.90040
NET.7FL.OZ.(207ML)
LOT NO

COCKTAILS

KIML

N (GRADE A) STEA

THREE CRABS Brand

ET HUONG FISHSAUCE COMPANY

Sauce
Phan Thiết

David Welch serves as maître d', bar manager, and co-owner of both Lincoln Restaurant and Sunshine Tavern, where his wife, Jenn Louis, is co-owner and chef. His cocktail menus nod to the classics with seasonal and playful twists. In creating this fish sauce Bloody Mary, Welch says: "We wanted to find a savory flavor that complements the richness of the tomato juice. In thinking about this, my mind went to Vietnamese noodle soup." In the restaurant, they prefer to shake theirs up with Red Boat sauce.

FISH SAUCE
BLOODY MARY

Owner/Bar Manager **DAVID WELCH** | **LINCOLN RESTAURANT** Portland, Oregon

FISH SAUCE
BLOODY MARY MIX

2½ cups tomato juice

5 tablespoons freshly squeezed lime juice

2 tablespoons fish sauce

¼ teaspoon salt

1 heaping tablespoon horseradish

¼ ounce olive juice

1 teaspoon Tabasco sauce

COCKTAIL

2 ounces vodka

Coarse salt, for rimming the glass

To make the Bloody Mary mix, combine the tomato juice, lime juice, fish sauce, salt, horseradish, olive juice, and Tabasco in a medium bowl. Whisk until completely incorporated. Any extra will keep for a few days in the refrigerator.

To make the cocktail, combine the vodka with 4 ounces of the Bloody Mary mix in a metal shaker filled with ice. Shake well, strain into a salt-rimmed pint glass, and serve.

MAKES 1 COCKTAIL

"Some version of this drink has been on every cocktail menu at every restaurant I have worked at in the last seven years," says Laurie Sheddan Harvey, the beverage and creative director at Houston's Sanctuari Bar. "I was inspired to re-create a version of a spicy drink that I got hooked on at a Thai restaurant in Montrose a decade ago. The drink constantly evolves, but the citrus and spicy flavors always remain." The addition of a little fish sauce in the Thai syrup adds a subtle savory note to this bold but well-balanced creation.

HANOI HIGH FIVE

Beverage and Creative Director **LAURIE SHEDDAN HARVEY** |
SANCTUARI BAR AT TRINITI Houston, Texas

THAI-INFUSED GREEN CHARTREUSE

5 Thai chiles
1 bottle green Chartreuse

MAKES 1 BOTTLE

THAI SYRUP

1 cup sugar
¼ cup peeled fresh ginger
4 stalks lemongrass, bruised to release flavor
⅛ teaspoon green curry paste
⅛ teaspoon fish sauce

MAKES 2 CUPS

HANOI HIGH FIVE

1½ ounces Fords gin
½ ounce freshly squeezed lime juice
½ ounce freshly squeezed lemon juice
Thai chile, for garnish
Lime wheel, for garnish

MAKES 1 COCKTAIL

To make the Thai-infused green Chartreuse, scorch the Thai chiles on a gas grill or by using a blow torch. Add the scorched peppers to a bottle of green Chartreuse and allow to infuse overnight. Strain out the peppers and seeds and discard.

To make the Thai syrup, bring 1 cup water to a boil. Turn off the heat and add the sugar, stirring until it has dissolved. While still hot, stir in the ginger, lemongrass, curry paste, and fish sauce. Let the syrup rest and cool before straining through a fine-mesh strainer. Store in a sealed squeeze bottle. The syrup will keep for up to 1 month in the refrigerator.

To make the Hanoi High Five, combine the gin, ½ ounce of the Chartreuse, the lime and lemon juices, and 1 ounce of the Thai syrup in a shaker with ice and shake. Strain into a coupe and garnish with a Thai chile and lime wheel.

Lara Nixon's passion for kitchen experimentation as a home cook is what inspired her to pursue a career in bar craft. She went on to become a spirits educator, author of the first children's book on bartending, and creator of Bad Dog Bar Craft artisanal bitters. Her culinary prowess shines through in this savory, tart cocktail. The carrot-pineapple shrub is equally enjoyable on its own, over ice, or mixed into the Saigon Shrub. For added depth, Nixon suggests swapping out a half ounce of tequila for mezcal. Or, for a virgin variation, replace the alcohol with a spicy ginger beer, such as Maine Root or Reed's. For a listing of locations and websites that carry Bad Dog Bar Craft bitters, visit www.baddogbarcraft.com.

SAIGON SHRUB

LARA NIXON | Spirits Educator and Owner of **BAD DOG BAR CRAFT** Austin, Texas

CARROT-PINEAPPLE SHRUB

4 cups fresh carrot juice

2½ cups pineapple juice

1¼ cups apple cider vinegar

⅔ cup honey

MAKES ABOUT 2 QUARTS

COCKTAIL

½ ounce fish sauce

1½ ounces tequila, or 1 ounce tequila and ½ ounce mezcal

2 dashes Bad Dog Bar Craft Fire & Damnation Bitters

MAKES 1 COCKTAIL

MOCKTAIL

½ ounce fish sauce

2 dashes Bad Dog Bar Craft Fire & Damnation Bitters

2 ounces ginger beer

MAKES 1 DRINK

To make the carrot-pineapple shrub, mix all the ingredients in a large bowl to combine. Store in covered glass jar or pitcher and place in the refrigerator for later enjoyment. The flavors will continue to harmonize over time. It will keep for 2 weeks and can be enjoyed over ice on its own.

To make the cocktail, mix together 4 ounces of the shrub, the fish sauce, and the tequila in a shaker. Add 2 dashes of bitters (or more, for a spicier variation) and stir with a bar spoon. Pour over ice in a rocks glass and serve.

To make the mocktail, mix together 4 ounces of the shrub and the fish sauce in a shaker. Add 2 dashes of bitters and stir with a bar spoon. Pour over ice in a rocks glass. Top with the ginger beer and serve.

ET HUONG FISHSAUCE COMPAN

THREE CRABS Brand

DESSERT

KIMI

AN (GRADE A) STEA

quid

BRAND

SH SAUCE

GREDIENTS:
Extract, Salt, Sugar.

roduct contains

sh (Anchovy)

Tim and Corey Sorenson, the ice cream magicians behind Cow Tipping Creamery in Austin, are known for their innovative sundaes using local and seasonal house-made toppings. They chose exotic Buddha's hand citrus for the base of their latest creation. "Its origin is traced back to the Far East, and it is a very fragrant fruit with lemon aroma that lacks the bitterness of other citrus and has no juice or pulp," explains Corey. "*Latik*—toasted coconut milk crumbs—are used in Filipino desserts, and I added the fish sauce to the final process to balance the sweetness of the *latik* and add a little of the salty-sweet component I was looking for to balance the sundae." This recipe can be made using a KitchenAid ice cream bowl attachment or any home ice cream maker. Buddha's hand appears around late summer/early fall, but citron or lemon may be substituted if it is out of season.

COCONUT BUDDHA'S HAND SUNDAE
WITH FISH SAUCE LATIK

Chef/Owners **TIM & COREY SORENSON** | **COW TIPPING CREAMERY** Austin, Texas

BUDDHA'S HAND ICE CREAM

2 (14-ounce) cans unsweetened coconut milk

1 cup sugar

1 cup half-and-half

Juice of 2 limes

Pinch of salt

½ cup Buddha's hand peel (a potato peeler can be used to create large zest chunks)

1 tablespoon cornstarch mixed with 2 tablespoons heavy cream

TOASTED COCONUT

2 cups sweetened shredded coconut

FISH SAUCE LATIK

1 (14-ounce) can unsweetened coconut milk

1 to 1½ teaspoons fish sauce

CANDIED BUDDHA'S HAND

1 Buddha's hand fruit

3 cups sugar

Continued

Before starting, make sure the ice cream bowl attachment has been in the freezer for at least 12 hours prior to freezing the ice cream.

To make the Buddha's hand ice cream, in a medium saucepan, whisk the coconut milk, sugar, half-and-half, lime juice, salt, and peel over medium heat until the sugar has dissolved and the mixture is simmering. Remove from the heat, add the slurry of cornstarch, and stir well. Transfer to a glass or ceramic bowl and cover with plastic wrap, then place in the refrigerator to cool overnight.

To make the toasted coconut, preheat the oven to 350°F. Toast the sweetened coconut on a rimmed baking sheet for 10 minutes. Remove and let cool before storing in an airtight container.

To make the *latik*, bring the coconut milk to a boil in a small saucepan over medium-high heat. Turn the heat down and gently simmer, whisking periodically, until the milk reduces to a thick cream, about 1 hour. Add the fish sauce and continue heating and stirring until the cream separates into coconut oil and solids. Turn off the heat as soon as the crumbs turn a deep caramel color. Drain the oil and store the remaining *latik* in an airtight container in the refrigerator to cool. The *latik* will keep for 1 month in the refrigerator. Leftovers may be sprinkled over any ice cream or used in a cake batter to add a sweet crunch.

To make the candied Buddha's hand, cut the fruit in half and place it flat-side down on a cutting board. Slice into ½-inch-wide sticks and dice the sticks into ½-inch cubes. Transfer the cubes of fruit to a medium saucepan and add the sugar and 3 cups water. Over medium heat, bring to a boil. Once boiling, lower the heat to a simmer and allow it to bubble slowly for about 1 hour. As the sugar reduces, the syrup will become thicker and the fruit will become translucent. The cooking is finished when the sugar reaches a temperature of 230 to 235°F. Once this temperature is reached, turn off the heat and let the fruit cool and rest for 30 minutes.

Strain the liquid into a bowl and reserve for later to pour over ice cream. Spread the fruit on a baking sheet lined with waxed or parchment paper and allow to dry overnight. Once cured, sprinkle with a little additional sugar to make it sparkle and store in a dark area, sealed in an airtight container.

To finish the ice cream, take the ice cream base out of the fridge, whisk again, and pour through a strainer to remove the Buddha's hand peel. Freeze in an ice cream maker according to manufacturer's directions. After about 15 minutes of freezing, add ½ cup of the candied fruit and ¼ cup of the *latik*. Transfer the ice cream to an airtight container with plastic wrap placed directly over the ice cream. Freeze for at least 3 hours for solid consistency.

To make a sundae, scoop the ice cream into a bowl and pour some of the reserved Buddha's hand simple syrup over it. Top with the candied fruit, *latik*, and toasted coconut.

MAKES ABOUT 10 SUNDAES

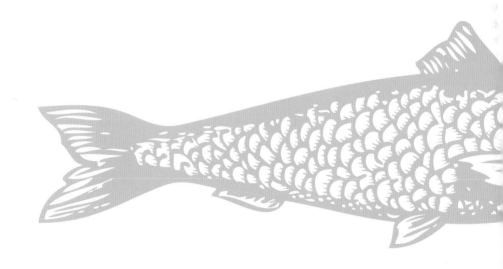

Chef Andrew Lewis is known for his remarkably innovative pastry creations at Austin's Uchi and Uchiko, as well as Uchi Houston. His diverse palette of flavors ranges from parsnip and barley to olives and hyssop. So, suffice it to say, using fish sauce as a pastry component was not all that far-fetched for him. "I'm always looking for new and different flavors and ingredients to incorporate into my desserts," says Lewis. "Being that Uchi is a modern sushi restaurant, fish sauce is something that we have on hand, yet rarely is it used in desserts." He was intrigued to discover the barrel-aged fish sauce collaboration between BLiS and Red Boat and recommends using it in this dish. And, while Uchiko makes their own toasted rice ice cream to accompany this dish, rice ice cream from the Asian market also works well.

APPLE FRITTERS
WITH FISH SAUCE APPLE MARMALADE

Executive Pastry Chef **ANDREW LEWIS** I **UCHIKO** Austin, Texas

APPLE FRITTER DOUGH

2¼ teaspoons (1 packet) active dry yeast

⅔ cup whole milk, warm (105 to 115°F)

3¼ cups plus 2 tablespoons all-purpose flour, divided

4 egg yolks

½ cup granulated sugar

⅓ cup apple cider

¼ cup (½ stick) unsalted butter, melted

1 tablespoon vanilla extract

1 teaspoon kosher salt

¼ teaspoon ground cinnamon

APPLES

¼ cup (½ stick) unsalted butter

1 vanilla bean

7 Granny Smith apples, peeled, cored, and chopped

¼ cup granulated sugar

1 cup apple cider

¼ cup apple cider vinegar

GLAZE

½ cup plus 2 tablespoons powdered sugar

¼ cup heavy cream

½ teaspoon vanilla extract

½ teaspoon kosher salt

APPLE LIQUID

About 1½ pounds green apples

1 teaspoon coarsely chopped shiso

1 tablespoon coarsely chopped fresh mint

½ cup freshly squeezed lime juice

⅓ cup very thinly sliced fresh ginger

1½ teaspoons finely sliced Thai chile

FISH SAUCE MARMALADE

1¾ cups granulated sugar

3 tablespoons ginger juice

¼ tablespoon kosher salt

Equal parts finely grated orange zest, fresh Thai basil, and shiso, finely chopped

1 tablespoon fish sauce

Rice ice cream, for serving

Fresh mint and Thai basil, for garnish

To make the apple fritter dough, place the yeast in a bowl. Pour the warm milk over the yeast and let it sit for 5 minutes. Add 2 cups of the flour, but do not stir. Cover the bowl with plastic wrap and set aside in a warm place until the surface of the flour cracks, 30 to 40 minutes.

In a medium bowl, whisk together the egg yolks and granulated sugar. Add the apple cider, butter, vanilla, salt, cinnamon, and 1¼ cups of the flour and whisk until combined. Then add to the yeast mixture. Using an electric mixer, beat the dough on low speed for 30 seconds, then increase the speed to medium and beat for 1 minute. Add the remaining 2 tablespoons flour and mix on low speed for 30 seconds, then increase to medium speed and beat for another 30 seconds. The dough will be very soft and sticky. Transfer the fritter dough to an oiled bowl, cover the bowl with plastic wrap, and set in a warm place until the dough has doubled in size, about 1½ hours.

To make the apples, melt the butter in a 12-inch skillet over medium heat. Slice the vanilla bean in half lengthwise and scrape the seeds into the pan with the melted butter. Drop the vanilla bean pod in, as well. Heat the butter until it is bubbling, then add the chopped apples, tossing to coat them with butter. Add the granulated sugar and cinnamon and cook for 5 minutes, stirring occasionally. Add the apple cider and vinegar, increasing the heat to medium-high, and cook until all the liquid has evaporated, stirring occasionally, 10 to 15 minutes. Remove the vanilla bean pod and transfer the apples to a baking sheet to cool.

To assemble the fritters, scrape the dough onto a well-floured surface and pat it into a 2-inch-thick 9 by 13-inch pan, flouring the surface as necessary. Spread half the apples over the dough, leaving space around the edges. Fold the dough into thirds (like a letter) by folding the bottom up and then the top down. Use your hands to again pat the dough into rectangle about 2 inches thick. Spread the remaining apples on top and fold into thirds again. Gather the dough together in a rough ball and return it to the oiled bowl. Cover and allow to rise until doubled in size, about 30 minutes.

Meanwhile, in a large Dutch oven, heat 3 to 4 inches of oil over medium heat to 375°F. Turn the dough out onto a well-floured surface and gently pat it out to ½-inch thickness, flouring the surface and the dough as necessary. Using a pizza cutter, bench scraper, or sharp knife, slice the dough into 1-inch pieces in a checkerboard pattern. Shape 4-ounce portions of the dough into round mounds and allow to rest for 10 minutes.

Continued

While the fritters are resting, make the glaze. Whisk together the powdered sugar, heavy cream, vanilla and salt in a medium bowl set over a small saucepan of simmering water over low heat. Heat and whisk occasionally until the mixture is warm to the touch. Remove from the heat and keep warm.

Very carefully drop each fritter into the hot oil, only adding as many as will comfortably fit in the pot so they are not crowded (4 or 5 at a time in a 7¼-quart Dutch oven). Fry until the underside is golden brown, about 3 minutes. Then, using a spatula, carefully turn them over and continue to cook until the other side is golden brown as well, another 4 to 5 minutes. Transfer the fritters to a paper towel–lined pan or a cooling rack. Repeat with the remaining dough, allowing the oil to come back up to temperature between batches. After removing each batch of fritters, allow them to sit for about 5 minutes, then brush with the glaze.

To make the apple liquid, combine the apples, *shiso,* mint, lime juice, ginger, Thai chile, and 5 cups water in a large pot and simmer over medium-low heat until thick. Purée in a food processor and strain through a coffee filter/cheesecloth for 12 hours in the fridge. (The best way to do this is to place a strainer over a deep bowl, put a coffee filter/cheesecloth over the strainer, and pour the apple liquid into filter-strainer setup.) Discard the solids. The apple liquid may be covered and refrigerated for up to 2 weeks. Leftover liquid can be used in sorbet or as a replacement for water in most bread recipes.

To make the fish sauce marmalade, combine 1 cup of the apple liquid, the sugar, ginger juice, salt, and ½ cup water in a small pot. Bring to a boil over medium-high heat, whisking occasionally, and cook until thick. Add equal parts of the orange zest, basil, and *shisho* to the marmalade. Add the fish sauce and stir to combine, seasoning with added fish sauce if desired. Store in a pint container or small bowl.

To assemble, tear each apple fritter into small pieces and place on a plate. Scoop the rice ice cream and place atop the apple fritters. Drizzle the fish sauce marmalade over the apple fritter pieces and ice cream. Garnish with mint and Thai basil before serving.

MAKES 8 FRITTERS

CONTRIBUTOR BIOGRAPHIES

Michelle Bernstein (page 88)

Chef Michelle Bernstein, a Miami native of Jewish and Latin descent, is a James Beard Award winner (Best Chef: South 2008) and author of *Cuisine a Latina* (Houghton Mifflin Harcourt, 2008). In collaboration with the renowned restaurant and entertainment collective KNR Hospitality, Bernstein (and her husband/business partner, David Martinez) are overseeing the food and beverage program at the hotel Thompson Miami Beach's restaurant Seagrape, an "old Florida"–style brasserie for which local farmers are growing unique fruits and vegetables. In addition, Martinez and Bernstein also own/operate Michelle Bernstein Catering Company, as well as her wildly popular café concept, Crumb on Parchment. She is currently developing a new concept to open in winter 2015 in the space that formerly housed her namesake restaurant, Michy's.

Spencer Bezaire (page 45)

Spencer Bezaire is a Los Angeles native who discovered his interest in cooking by watching his Japanese grandmother cook and witnessing his mother's love of growing seasonal produce. Shortly after high school, Bezaire attended Le Cordon Bleu in Pasadena, California. While there, he interned at popular brasserie Café Stella in Silver Lake. Upon graduating in 2008, he quickly worked his way up to become the executive chef, where he formed close relationships with farmers and brought a fresh, seasonal French menu to the table. At Café Stella, Bezaire met Dustin Lancaster, and in 2012, they opened L&E Oyster Bar with Tyler Bell. Bezaire serves as the executive chef and has developed a seasonal, seafood-driven menu. He is continuously building close relationships with oyster farmers up and down the East and West Coasts, bringing the freshest, most coveted oysters to Los Angeles and creating local, seasonal cuisine for the neighborhood. In 2014, Bezaire returned to Sunset Junction in Silver Lake to open El Condor with Lancaster.

Ho Chee Boon (page 80)

Chef Ho Chee Boon, Hakkasan's international executive chef, is responsible for new openings and menu development around the world, with a focus on creating new dishes for specific locations using the finest local ingredients. After moving to the United States in 2012 to launch Hakkasan New York, Chef Ho was awarded a Michelin star within eight months of opening. He has since headed up all subsequent U.S. openings, including San Francisco, Las Vegas, and Los Angeles, as well as overseeing operations as far afield as Dubai, Mumbai, and Doha. In a career spanning twenty-six years, Chef Ho has worked for some of the world's most renowned Asian restaurants, including the East Ocean Restaurant in Hong Kong, Breeze at the five-star Lebua Bangkok, Singapore's exclusive Temasek Club, and Moscow's premier dining venue, Turandot. He now divides his time between Las Vegas (where he helms the flagship restaurant at the iconic MGM Grand) and San Francisco, where some of the finest produce grown in the United States inspires his development of Hakkasan's culinary repertoire.

Stuart Brioza (page 85)

Stuart Brioza, chef/owner of State Bird Provisions in San Francisco, attended the Culinary Institute of America in Hyde Park, New York, where he graduated with top honors. He launched his cooking career in the 1990s, working for Chef John Hogan in Chicago at Savarin. In the spring of 2000, Stuart was hired to be the executive chef and pastry chef at Tapawingo in Ellsworth, Michigan. In 2003, Stuart was named one of *Food & Wine* magazine's 10 Best New Chefs of America for his technique and commitment to using the best local ingredients. In 2004, Stuart and his wife, Nicole, who is a pastry chef, were recruited by restaurateur Drew Nieporent and master sommelier Larry Stone to take over the kitchen at Rubicon in San Francisco. In less than a year, their cooking re-established the decade-old restaurant as one of the top dining destinations in San Francisco, garnering numerous local and international accolades. In 2011, Stuart and Nicole opened the award-winning State Bird Provisions, which has received the following recognition and accolades: *Bon Appétit* magazine's Best New Restaurant of 2012; *Food & Wine* magazine's Best Chef All-Stars 2013; James Beard Award: Best New Restaurant 2013; Tasting Table Best Pastry Chefs of 2013; *San Francisco* magazine's Best Chefs 2013; Zagat: The 10 Hottest Restaurants in the World; *San Francisco Chronicle*: Top 100 Restaurants 2012–13; *San Francisco Business Journal* Forty Under 40, Class of 2013; *7x7* magazine: Eat + Drink Awards 2013 and 2014; one Michelin star, 2014 and 2015 *Michelin Guide*. In 2014, they opened The Progress, their latest and highly anticipated family-style restaurant concept.

Alexis Chong (page 82)

Growing up in the north Bay Area of California, Alexis was exposed to many different types of foods, such as the abalone and sea urchin that her father would bring home after a dive. Alexis's career in the restaurant business began with a dishwashing job at Barnacle Billy's in Ogunquit, Maine, where at age fifteen she graduated to busgirl. She later entered the Art Institute of Seattle and attended the School of Culinary Arts. Her externship while at the institute led her to a job working with Chef Michael Mina at Aqua in San Francisco. She later returned to Seattle

and the Skamania Lodge in Stevenson, Washington. Visiting Austin on a whim, a job at the Driskill Grill presented itself, and soon she was introduced to Executive Chef Rene Ortiz of La Condesa. Starting as a grill cook at La Condesa, she was promoted to co-sous chef. In mid-2012, Alexis joined Ortiz as the chef de cuisine at Sway, where she was promoted a year later—when Sway was named one of *Bon Appétit*'s 50 Best New Restaurants in America.

Leah Cohen (page 39)

A graduate of the Culinary Institute of America in Hyde Park, New York, Leah's first position was working for celebrated chef David Burke at Park Avenue Café in New York. While there, she adapted David's philosophy of utilizing the freshest seasonal ingredients and was encouraged to enroll in a Slow Food program based in Italy. After studying the intricacies of Italy's diverse culinary landscape, Leah stayed on for an additional year in Sicily at the Michelin-starred restaurant La Madia, to focus on a cuisine that blends the bold and fresh flavors of the Mediterranean. Upon returning to New York, Leah refined her craft at Eleven Madison Park under the tutelage of Chef Daniel Humm. After working for a year at the four-star restaurant, Leah traded in refined for rustic when she joined Anne Burrell at Centro Vinoteca in 2008. While working under Chef Burrell, Leah further explored her love of Italian cooking and appeared on season five on Bravo's *Top Chef*. After a successful run on the show and with national recognition, Leah returned to Centro Vinoteca as the restaurant's executive chef. After a few years there, she decided to take a sabbatical and travel throughout Southeast Asia to learn about her Asian heritage. One year later, Leah returned home to bring the bold flavors of Asian street food to New York by opening Pig & Khao on the Lower East Side.

Gerard Craft (page 56)

A native of Washington, D.C., Chef Gerard Craft became addicted to the restaurant life while living in Salt Lake City as a snowboard photographer. Chef Craft went on to cook at Bistro Toujours in Park City, Utah, and Chateau Marmont in Los Angeles, California, as well as a stage at Ryland Inn in Whitehouse Station, New Jersey, before making the leap to open a restaurant of his own. After opening Niche in 2005 at the age of twenty-five, Chef Craft extended his restaurant group to include Taste by Niche, a modern speakeasy; Brasserie by Niche, a classic French bistro; and his latest Italian concept, Pastaria. Chef Craft's creative yet simple food has earned him recognition as a *Food & Wine* Best New Chef and as one of *Inc.* magazine's Star Entrepreneurs under 30. He is also a five-time James Beard Foundation finalist for Best Chef: Midwest.

Jason Dady (page 42)

Jason Dady is chef/owner of the Jason Dady Restaurant Group in San Antonio, Texas. The group is composed of a wide array of concepts including Umai Mi, Tre Trattoria, Two Bros BBQ Market, B&D Ice House, The DUK Truck, and Jason Dady Catering and Events. Jason's genuine passions for innovative flavors and old-fashioned hospitality have propelled him into a career as a chef, restaurateur, entrepreneur, and San Antonio culinary staple. With thirteen years of success and a James Beard semifinalist nomination, he continues to provide superior dining experiences. His dedication and talent have earned him titles such as Best Chefs in America, Star Chef Restaurateur by StarChefs, New Achiever Award, and Rising Star chef recognition, as well as cover photos on *Restaurant Hospitality* and *NSIDE* magazines.

Vinny Dotolo & Jon Shook (page 77)

Los Angeles chefs Vinny Dotolo and Jon Shook are the owners of animal, Son of a Gun, Trois Mec, and Petit Trois. Their partnership began more than a decade ago when they met in culinary school at the Art Institute of Fort Lauderdale. While at school, they worked for Michelle Bernstein at The Strand and Mark's Place by Mark Militello, and after graduation, they traveled west and worked at The Wildflower in Vail, Colorado. In 2002, they landed in Los Angeles and worked at Chadwick for Benjamin Ford and Govind Armstrong, which would inspire them to launch their initial catering company, Caramelized Productions. Caramelized Productions was a huge success, paving the way for their own TV show on the Food Network plus an award-winning cookbook. In 2008, they opened animal, and then Son of a Gun in 2011. Shook and Dotolo's most recent venture was a partnership with French chef Ludo Lefebvre: Together they opened the highly acclaimed Trois Mec in 2013 and Petit Trois in 2014. Shook and Dotolo have received numerous nominations and awards including *Food & Wine*'s 2009 Best New Chef, StarChefs' 2008 Rising Star Chef, and four James Beard nominations, including 2009's Best New Restaurant for animal, 2011's Best Chef: Pacific, and Best Chef: West in 2013 and 2014.

Todd Duplechan (page 64)

Born and raised in Richardson, Texas, Todd Duplechan, co-owner and executive chef of Lenoir and co-owner of Métier's Cook Supply alongside wife Jessica Maher, was exposed to a wide range of cuisines as a child, which piqued his interest in cooking. Duplechan worked at Solly's BBQ in Dallas as a teenager before making the move to Colorado, where he originally had his sights set on being an architect. Instead, he received his associate's degree from the Art Institute of Denver's culinary school, and upon graduation, worked under a sushi master for two years at Tommy Tsunami's in Denver, then as a sous chef at Sambuca. Expanding his horizons, Duplechan traveled in Europe for six months, where he worked at an olive farm in Tuscany and in guest services in Corfu, Greece, before moving to Grand Cayman, where he took on the position of a hotel chef. A year and a half later, Duplechan returned stateside to New York City to work at Danube and Tabla, and eventually was executive sous chef under James Beard–nominated Dan Kluger at The Core Club. Duplechan moved to Austin, Texas, where he was hired as the opening chef of the Four Seasons Hotel's Trio restaurant, until he and his wife opened Lenoir in 2012 and Métier's Cook Supply in August 2014.

Kresha Faber (page 4)

Kresha Faber is the author and editor of *Nourishing Joy*, a website dedicated to real food, sustainable living, natural homemaking, and joyful parenting. She is passionate about sharing ways to make small, simple changes to live more healthily, frugally, and sustainably. Kresha is the author of *The DIY Pantry* and the e-book *Restocking the Pantry*. You can visit her website at www.nourishingjoy.com.

Dylan Fultineer (page 7)

Originally from York, Pennsylvania, Dylan Fultineer developed his lifelong interest in food from watching his Pennsylvania Dutch relatives cure meats and make sauerkraut. He apprenticed under James Beard Award–winning Chef Paul Kahan at Blackbird in Chicago from 1999 to 2006. While there, the *Chicago Tribune* named him one of the top three sous chefs in the city. He then moved to Los Angeles to run the kitchen at the second location of The Hungry Cat (by another James Beard Award winner, Chef Suzanne Goin) and cook for the brewpub at Hollister Brewing Co. Before opening Rappahannock in 2012, the executive chef first helped overhaul the menu at Merroir restaurant in Topping, Virginia, and designed the menu for Rappahannock Oyster Bar in Washington, D.C. Featured in the *Washingtonian* magazine as one of the Top 10 Restaurant Openings of 2012, Rappahannock Oyster Bar was also cited in the *Wall Street Journal* as one of Five Outstanding Oyster Bars Around the Country and was most recently named one of the Best New Restaurants of 2014 by *Esquire*.

Matthew Gaudet (page 66)

Chef Matthew Gaudet was drawn to his first restaurant job at the early age of fifteen, washing dishes part-time in order to save money for his first car. While training at the Cambridge School of Culinary Arts, Gaudet worked in the Cambridge, Massachusetts, mainstay Chez Henri. Soon thereafter, he took a position at the prestigious Eleven Madison Park during its opening year. From there, he continued to hone his craft, moving to Jean-Georges before returning to Eleven Madison to become sous chef within Danny Meyer's Union Square Hospitality Group. A few years later, he was tapped to be a sous chef at Aquavit under award-winning chef Marcus Samuelsson, then a sous chef for 71 Clinton, and finally a sous chef for Tocqueville. After nine years in the Big Apple, he took on the position of chef de cuisine at Brasserie Jo in Boston, working directly with Jean Joho to help captain the 200-seat institution. In 2009, he joined the team at the Aquitaine Group, where he served as chef de cuisine of the original Aquitaine in the South End. In the spring of 2012, Gaudet opened West Bridge with partner Alexis Gelburd-Kimler. In its first year, West Bridge and Chef Gaudet received a three and a half out of four star review from the *Boston Globe*; West Bridge was also named one of the 12 Best New Restaurants by *GQ's* Alan Richman and one of the Top 50 New Restaurants of 2013 by *Bon Appétit*. In 2013 *Food & Wine* magazine named Gaudent as one of its Best New Chefs.

Jack Gilmore (page 19)

Jack Gilmore began his culinary career working with "old school" Cajun chefs in South Padre Island, Texas. Seeking new challenges, Gilmore relocated to Austin, where he helped open the original Chez Fred's and longtime seafood favorite Louie's on the Lake before moving to Louisiana. Returning to Texas in the mid-1980s, Chef Gilmore worked under German chefs in Fredericksburg, which truly helped shape his culinary vision. Gilmore returned to Austin in 1990 to create the culinary vision for the legendary Z'Tejas Grill. Here he was the founding executive chef, and fresh ingredients and signature elements marked his distinctive style. In October 2009, Jack and managing partner Tom Kamm left Z'Tejas to create their dream project—Jack Allen's Kitchen, a restaurant focusing on fresh farm-to-table ingredients, spirited Texas cuisine, and true Southern hospitality. Since the opening of Jack Allen's Kitchen Oak Hill in 2009, Gilmore and Kamm have opened a location in Round Rock, and a third location is scheduled to open in Westlake in early 2015. Committed to Texas farmers and purveyors, Gilmore has pledged himself and his restaurants to support the community—no matter what the ups and downs of working with Mother Nature may be.

Michael Gulotta (page 10)

Born and raised in New Orleans, Chef Michael Gulotta graduated from Nicholls State University in Thibodaux, Louisiana, with a bachelor's degree in culinary arts. While pursuing his studies, Michael made his way through the ranks of Chef Folse's highly touted Lafitte's Landing Restaurant, where he mastered the fundamentals of Creole and Cajun cuisines. Upon graduation, he moved back to New Orleans, where he rose through the brigade at Restaurant August under the tutelage of Chef John Besh. Chef Gulotta was encouraged by his new mentor to pursue his culinary studies abroad, where he would live, learn, and cook on the Italian Riviera at Restaurant Giunchetto, then apprentice in the mountains of the Black Forest in Germany under Chef Karl-Josef Fuchs. After years in Germany, Hurricane Katrina hit, and Gulotta returned home to help rebuild not only his childhood home but also his beloved New Orleans. In 2007, Chef Gulotta was promoted to chef de cuisine of August, where he remained until 2013, earning consistently positive reviews and solidifying Restaurant August as the benchmark of fine dining in the South. In 2014, Michael opened Southeast Asian–inspired MoPho in New Orleans's Mid-City with his brother Jeff Gulotta and business partner Jeffrey Bybee.

Laurie Sheddan Harvey (page 94)

Laurie started her formal restaurant profession after a career as an emergency room trauma nurse. It was a move to Reno (where she started one of the original female bank track derby leagues in the country, called the Reno Roller Girls) that prompted her to find a bartending gig. There, she found that her strong organizational skills and affinity for chemistry, which worked in a trauma room, helped her quickly rise up the bartending ranks. A return to her native Houston found Laurie working and managing some of Houston's favored establishments and watering holes—Dolce Vita, Beaver's, Haven, and Philippe. Laurie took over the beverage program at Triniti in 2013. She and her talented team of bartenders spend much of their time in Triniti's kitchen creating the shrubs, infusions, syrups, and tinctures that are the building blocks of flavor in the cocktails on the menu at Sanctuari Bar.

Linton Hopkins (page 52)

Linton Hopkins is an internationally celebrated chef with deep Atlanta roots. A graduate of Emory University and the Culinary Institute of America, Hopkins honed his culinary skills at restaurants in New Orleans and Washington, D.C., before returning to Georgia to open Restaurant Eugene with his wife, Gina, in 2004. Since then, the couple has gone on to open Holeman, Finch Public House, and other beloved restaurants around Atlanta. Chef Hopkins has garnered national attention and accolades for his from-scratch cookery, including the James Beard Award for Best Chef: Southeast in 2012. He is in constant pursuit of deliciousness, coaxing flavors from the highest quality ingredients sourced from artisans and farmers in his backyard and across the globe.

Michael Hung (page 50)

Michael Hung began his culinary career in New York City, taking on extended stages at acclaimed restaurants Daniel and Aquavit in lieu of finishing culinary school. He followed his heart to San Francisco in 2005 and joined Traci Des Jardins's James Beard Award–winning team at Jardiniere before going on to work at other Bay Area restaurants, including a stint as executive chef of Bushi-tei and chef de cuisine at Roland Passot's La Folie, a Michelin-starred restaurant that received four stars from the *San Francisco Chronicle*. In addition to his work at La Folie, he also founded and ran the philanthropic pop-up dinner series Red Sparrow. In December 2013, Hung joined the team at Coastal Luxury Management to become the executive chef of its newest restaurant, Faith & Flower, which is located in downtown Los Angeles and opened in 2014. Hung had the opportunity to work on Pixar's Academy Award–winning animated movie *Ratatouille*, earning himself a film credit as "menu chef" and consultant, alongside legendary chefs Thomas Keller and Guy Savoy.

Stephanie Izard (page 8)

Stephanie Izard is a graduate of the University of Michigan and the Scottsdale Culinary Institute and has worked in some of the most respected kitchens in Chicago, including La Tache, Spring, and Vong. She previously owned the highly acclaimed restaurant Scylla, which she sold just prior to appearing on and winning season four of Bravo's *Top Chef*. Izard was the first woman to win in 2008 and is the only winner of the original version of the show to take the title of Fan Favorite. Izard's first book, *Girl in the Kitchen*, was released in 2011. A 2011 James Beard Best New Restaurant nominee, Girl & the Goat has been praised by high-profile publications such as *Saveur*, the *New York Times*, *Food & Wine*, *Better Homes and Gardens*, and others. Little Goat, Stephanie's highly successful follow-up to Girl & the Goat, encompasses a diner, coffee shop, bread shop, and bar. An outpost of Little Goat Bakery opened at the Chicago French Market in Spring 2013. Izard was named one of *Food & Wine*'s Best New Chefs in 2011 and received a James Beard Award for Best Chef: Great Lakes in 2013. In 2014, she was inducted into the Chicago Culinary Museum and Chefs Hall of Fame.

Matt Jennings (page 79)

With three consecutive James Beard Foundation Award nominations for Best Chef: Northeast, three Cochon 555 wins, and a spot on *Food & Wine*'s Forty Under 40 Big Thinkers in America list, Chef Matt Jennings is recognized nationally for his bold, lusty cooking and dedication to New England locality through artisan and seasonal ingredients. A Boston native and graduate of the New England Culinary Institute in Vermont, Jennings started his career in notable American and European kitchens before leading the specialty sourcing programs at Cowgirl Creamery and Tomales Bay Foods (San Francisco) and Formaggio Kitchen (Cambridge, Massachusetts), where he met his wife, Kate Jennings. In 2002, the pair opened Farmstead, an artisan food and cheese shop in Providence, Rhode Island. In 2006, Jennings introduced Farmstead's adjacent bistro, leading to a decade of national acclaim. Jennings closed Farmstead in June 2014, returning to his native Boston to focus on Townsman, a new restaurant opening in 2015. Located in the new Radian Building at 120 Kingston Street in downtown Boston, Townsman will pay homage to Jennings's New England roots, showcasing his commitment to the region's ingredients, purveyors, and traditions.

Edward Kim (page 26)

Born and raised in Chicago's northwest suburbs, Chef Edward Kim attended New York University, earning a B.A. in political science with the intention of one day becoming an attorney. Taking a turn in the more creative direction, Chef Kim enrolled in Pasadena's Le Cordon Bleu, where he discovered his passion for food and cooking and graduated with a culinary degree. After culinary school, Chef Kim honed his skills in various New York and Los

Angeles kitchens under a number of acclaimed chefs and other respected individuals in the culinary community. He served as chef de cuisine at Elements Catering (Pasadena, California); commis during an externship at Per Se; and garde manager at Meson G (Los Angeles). In 2011, Chef Kim opened his first restaurant, Ruxbin, in Chicago's Wicker Park neighborhood. Immediately, Ruxbin garnered national attention, earning the honor of Best New Restaurant from both *GQ* and *Bon Appétit* magazines. Two years later, Chef Kim and his partners opened their second concept, Mott St, a more casual restaurant that showcases family-style fare in a relaxed environment. His restaurants have been honored with awards and accolades from Michelin, *Bon Appétit*, the *New York Times*, *Food & Wine*, *GQ*, *Details*, and the *Chicago Tribune*. He crafts a straightforward yet progressive menu drawing from his extensive culinary background, classic French training, Asian heritage, and widespread travels.

Amy Kritzer (page 70)

Amy Kritzer is a recipe developer, food writer, and founder of the cooking website *What Jew Wanna Eat*. She puts a modern spin on traditional Jewish recipes, such as her Tex Mex Potato Latkes or Chocolate Hazelnut Rugelach, on her popular site. Her recipes and writing have been featured in numerous media venues including the *Today* show, *Cosmopolitan*, and *Bon Appétit*. In 2012, she was a finalist in Daily Candy's Start Small Go Big small business competition, and in 2013, *Relish* magazine named her a Top 5 Jewish Blogger. Follow her at www.whatjewwannaeat.com.

Jiyeon Lee (page 90)

Born in southern South Korea and raised in Seoul, Jiyeon has brought her family heritage and cultural influences to the Atlanta dining scene. Once a K-Pop singing star, Chef Lee now concentrates on how she can combine her past food memories with her current surroundings. After cooking at ZUMA, Repast, and Hotel St. Regis

in Atlanta, she and husband Cody Taylor opened Heirloom Market BBQ in 2010 and Sobban in 2013. Both restaurants merge the flavors and techniques of the East with those of the American South.

Mary Helen Leonard (page 22)

Mary Helen Leonard is a lifestyle writer and culinary instructor living in Austin, Texas. She began her culinary studies while living in Beijing, and later attended the Community Culinary School of Northwestern Connecticut to complete her education. Mary Helen has long since left the restaurant business for a life of writing, teaching, and motherhood. When she's not in the kitchen, she enjoys cooking indulgent meals at home, blogging her brains out, and dreaming of new and interesting places to visit. Follow her at www.MaryMakesGood.com.

Evan LeRoy (page 69)

Evan LeRoy manned the pits at Hill Country Barbecue in New York City before returning to his hometown of Austin, Texas, where he attended culinary school at Le Cordon Bleu. His experience ranges from crafting tacos at Torchy's to cooking upscale, ranch-inspired cuisine at Hudson's on the Bend. He is currently the pit master and head chef at Freedmen's.

Andrew Lewis (page 102)

Born and raised in the Lone Star state, Andrew Lewis originally had his eye on the law and spent two years pursuing a bachelor's degree in law enforcement. But influence from his father's cooking hobby and his own love for chocolate and sweets drew him into the kitchen. In order to realize this passion, Lewis enrolled in a local culinary school but realized not long after that he would prefer to learn in the hands-on environment of a kitchen. He began his career at Eatzi's Market and Bakery, quickly rising through the ranks to take full responsibility for the bakery production. After working his way through a several bakeries, he launched his restaurant career, first at the small

French restaurant Mignon and then at Bolla in the Stoneleigh Hotel, working under 2012 Austin Rising Star Chef David Bull. Bolla gave Lewis the chance to learn about fine dining, plating, and refinement. Eventually he applied those skills at Stephan Pyles's namesake restaurant before moving to Austin, where he accepted a position at Uchiko as head pastry chef. In 2014, he was named executive pastry chef of the Uchi restaurants: Uchi, Uchiko, and Uchi Houston. He lives in Austin and continues to pursue ground-breaking desserts, showcasing familiar flavors in completely original forms and combinations.

Jeremy Lieb (page 9)

As the newly appointed executive chef of Boca in Cincinnati, Ohio, Chef Jeremy Lieb brings his years of experience at restaurants across the globe to the European-inspired menu. Born in Las Vegas, Lieb received his culinary degree from Milwaukee Area Technical College. After completing school, Lieb moved to Cincinnati and began cooking at La Maisonette, the nation's longest-running five-star Mobil restaurant. At La Maisonette, Lieb met Boca owner David Falk, as well as his future wife, Chef Bridget Eagan. Under mentor and La Maisonette owner Jean-Robert de Cavel, Lieb went on to train at three-star Michelin restaurant Bernard L'Oiseau in the Côte D'Or, France. While in France, Lieb fell in love with French technique and upon his return was offered a chef de partie position with Chef Daniel Boulud in New York, working at Daniel and Café Boulud and helping develop the restaurant's first cookbook. Lieb went back to his hometown of Las Vegas, where he held chef and executive chef positions at Le Cirque, The Mansion at MGM Grand, and Restaurant Medici at the Ritz-Carlton, which *Food & Wine* went on to name one of the 25 Best Restaurants in America. After his success in Las Vegas, Lieb headed to Atlanta where he opened Trois, a modern French restaurant named Best New Restaurant by *Esquire* magazine and Restaurant of the Year by *Atlanta* magazine. With

an offer to go back to Cincinnati, he held a position as corporate chef with the Jeff Ruby Group before returning to his French roots with Boca Restaurant Group, where he now oversees the kitchen as executive chef.

Mei Lin (page 60)

Mei grew up working alongside her father at their family-owned-and-operated restaurant outside Detroit, where she learned the fundamentals of being a well-rounded cook and running a restaurant. Throughout the years she has had the privilege of working for some of the most revered chefs in the industry, such as Michael Symon (Roast), Marcus Samuelsson (C-House), and Wolfgang Puck, whose company provided much of her early training and refinement of skills during her three-year involvement. After cutting her teeth at Spago Las Vegas, she eventually moved to West Hollywood to join Michael Voltaggio's opening team at ink. in Los Angeles. She spent the last three years there moving up the ranks to eventually become a sous chef at the critically acclaimed establishment before going on to compete on *Top Chef*, where she was named winner of season twelve.

Kevin Luzande (page 36)

A native Angeleno, Kevin Luzande was raised in the San Fernando Valley, where he began assisting his parents, both Filipino immigrants, with the household cooking at an early age. Luzande went on to attend the Le Cordon Bleu–affiliated California School of Culinary Arts in Pasadena, graduating in 2002. He completed an externship at the Ritz-Carlton Marina del Rey under the direction of Chef Troy Thompson before taking the opportunity to run the kitchen of celebrity chef David Burke's restaurant in Las Vegas. When he returned to Los Angeles in 2009, Luzande worked with Chef John Sedlar (the acclaimed pioneer of modern Latin cuisine) at his restaurant Rivera. Beginning as sous chef, he quickly ascended to chef de cuisine. Two years later, Sedlar appointed Luzande as opening chef de cuisine at his new restaurant, Playa, where he worked until the establishment closed in 2013. Last June, Luzande reunited with his mentor when he accompanied Sedlar to France, representing the United States at the biannual Fête le Vin in Bordeaux, a sister city of Los Angeles. Until most recently, Luzande was chef de cuisine at Acabar in Hollywood, working under Chef Octavio Becerra. Their diverse dishes married French culinary techniques with the exotic cuisines of the Mediterranean and North Africa, the Middle East, India, Indochina, and Southeast Asia.

Veronica Meewes (page 23)

Veronica Meewes has been fascinated with food since her early days of kitchen experimentation growing up in New Jersey. She studied writing and sociology at Sarah Lawrence College in New York before moving to Austin, Texas, where she specializes in food, beverage, travel, and lifestyle features. She has been writing for both digital and print publications since 2005, and her work has appeared in *Forbes Travel Guide*, *Food & Wine*, *TODAY* Food, *Tasting Table*, *GOOD*, *Serious Eats*, *Texas Highways*, *Austin Monthly*, the *Austin-American Statesman*, *Citygram Austin*, and more. Veronica is a member of the Austin Food Blogger Alliance and a home cook mentor for foster youth through the nonprofit Fresh Chefs Society. Follow her adventures at www.veronicameewes.com and on Instagram and Twitter @wellfedlife.

Lara Nixon (page 96)

Lara Nixon is a home chef whose love of various culinary traditions inspired her to begin working in bar craft. She has since become a bar consultant; spirits educator; author of *A Is for Absinthe*; and the founder of Bad Dog Bar Craft, a line of artisanal bitters based out of Austin, Texas.

Chris Pandel (page 48)

Chris Pandel began his career as a chef by working in restaurants in his hometown of Riverside, Illinois, before attending Johnson and Wales University and interning at Chicago chef-factory Tru under Chef Rick Tramonto. Pandel spent what he calls "graduate school" in New York, at Café Boulud under Chef Andrew Carmellini. Love of home brought him back to Chicago and Tru, which led to a position as corporate chef at three Tramonto restaurants. Of his mentors, Pandel says Carmellini molded him into a cook, and that under Tramonto, he earned a "sense of self" in the kitchen and the know-how to run a business. In 2008, Pandel opened neighborhood eatery The Bristol with partners John Ross and Phillip Waters. His second restaurant, Balena, which opened in 2012, made *Bon Appétit*'s list of 25 Best New Restaurants in 2012 and was nominated for a James Beard Best New Restaurant award. In 2015, he will open Formento's, which will pay tribute to 1950s Italian American red sauce joints. Another restaurant he will open is Armour & Swift, which will feature a meat-centric menu celebrating the history of Chicago's meatpacking district.

Ryan Pera (page 28)

After cooking in New York City at Le Cirque and as chef de cuisine to Jonathan Waxman, Houston native Ryan Pera first captured the attention of diners at 17 Restaurant in the Alden Hotel, where his modern American menu was praised by the *Houston Chronicle*. But it was at Revival Market, which he opened with partner Morgan Weber in 2011, where his serious commitment to sourcing the best local ingredients at their peak and using every leaf, berry, and nose-to-tail cut made him a household name in the greater Houston culinary scene. Ryan's mastery of all things cured, hung, and stuffed into casings has become the showcase of the Market, which has been featured in national publications from the *New York Times* and the *Wall Street Journal* to *Food & Wine* magazine. In 2012, *Bon Appétit* magazine named Revival Market one of Five Best Artisanal Butchers in America. In early 2014, Pera and Weber opened Coltivare, where they've designed a menu to utilize their garden bounty to create dishes that are true to the Italian cooking philosophy while reflecting the chef's American sensibility and signature style. Coltivare was named one of the Top 50 New Restaurants of 2014 by *Bon Appétit* magazine.

Annie Pettry (page 32)

Growing up in Asheville, North Carolina, Annie Pettry's childhood was steeped in influential food experiences, including growing vegetables, foraging for mushrooms, trout fishing, and countless hours in the kitchen learning from her parents' global cooking style. Through her twenties, she worked in myriad restaurant roles before enrolling at the International Culinary Center in New York, where she earned a grand diploma in culinary arts. After finishing her formal education, she worked alongside numerous renowned chefs, including Craig Koketsu (Quality Meats, New York City), Elliott Moss (The Admiral, Asheville), and Loretta Keller (Moss Room, San Francisco). As the Decca team tirelessly scouted talent from coast to coast, it was ultimately Keller who recommended Pettry for the coveted role of executive chef at this Louisville, Kentucky, hotspot when it opened in 2012.

Kim and Hong Pham (page 72)

Los Angeles–based Kim and Hong Pham are the couple behind the food blog *The Ravenous Couple*. They are both self-taught home cooks but learned much from their families along the way. Raised in first-generation immigrant Vietnamese American families in opposite parts of the country, they were both nurtured with a love for Vietnamese culture and heritage, which they strive to spread and preserve with the recipes on their site, started in 2009. Follow them at www.theravenouscouple.com.

Monica Pope (page 6)

German-born, Texas-reared chef Monica Pope has been revolutionizing Houston's culinary scene since she debuted her first restaurant in 1992. Pope shares her passion for connecting local farmers and consumers with cooking classes, an online cookbook *Eat Where Your Food Lives*, plus Sparrow Bar + Cookshop and Beaver's restaurants. Pope has enjoyed national recognition from a James Beard Award nomination and a spot competing on season two of Bravo's *Top Chef Masters*. She is the only female Texas chef to be named Best New Chef by *Food & Wine* magazine thanks to her inventive, "eat where your food lives" cooking style. Hailed by *Travel & Leisure* magazine as "one of the most ingenious restaurateurs around," Pope first learned to cook from her Czech grandmother and went on to earn her chef's title from Leiths School of Food and Wine in London. After working in Europe and San Francisco, she returned home to Houston to open the Quilted Toque, which was followed by a succession of acclaimed restaurants, including Boulevard Bistro and t'afia. Pope is the advisory board founding chair and current board member of Recipe for Success, a Houston-based nonprofit that is dedicated to fighting childhood obesity.

Chris Shepherd (page 44)

In 2012, Midwest-raised chef Chris Shepherd opened Underbelly, featuring locally sourced food inspired by the ethnic diversity of Houston. The Art Institute alum and former executive sous chef-turned-sommelier of Brennan's brings his farm-to-table passion to fruition at Underbelly, which sources ingredients from the Gulf Coast, surrounding farms, and ranches. The in-house butcher shop, which only uses whole animal, supports Shepherd's passion for butchering and charcuterie. This 2014 James Beard Award winner for Best Chef: Southwest was also named one of the Top 10 Best New Chefs in America by *Food & Wine*. Underbelly was named one of the best new restaurants in the country by *Bon Appétit* and *Esquire* and one of the seventy best new restaurants in the world by *Condé Nast Traveler*. In 2013, Chris opened two Underbelly kiosks inside Reliant Stadium to serve three signature dishes during Houston Texans (NFL) home games.

Corey and Tim Sorensen (page 98)

Corey Sorensen is a trained jewelry designer and graduate of New York's Fashion Institute of Technology. She is a self-taught soft-serve ice cream dessert designer who creates and combines unusual and creative soft-serve profiles with baked goods and toppings to make a truly unique ice cream dessert experience. Timothy Sorensen, also a graduate of FIT, has been married to Corey for more than twenty years. His background mostly in graphics has lead him to jobs as varied as post production coordinator for Pixar Animation to managing the custom motorcycles company Flyrite Choppers. He oversees the daily workings of Cow Tipping Creamery's truck, designs the graphics, and manages the business end. In 2012, after years of coast-to-coast ice cream research and development, the two opened Cow Tipping Creamery in Austin. Using the best ingredients they can find, they translate hard scoop into soft serve by infusing their dairy with fresh herbs, fruits, coffee, and nuts. They also offer an array of homemade toppings and baked goods to complement their innovative ice cream creations.

David Swanson (page 34)

David began working in restaurant kitchens at the age of sixteen and soon realized what wonders could be created with food. He trained at the Culinary School of Kendall College (Evanston, Illinois) and Le Cordon Bleu in Paris that same year. He worked at Le Titi de Paris under the tutelage of Pierre Pollin, followed by Commander's Palace in New Orleans, where he broadened his culinary scope by learning American regional cooking and understanding the importance of local, indigenous products. Upon returning to the Midwest, David worked for Don Yamauchi

at Carlos' Restaurant, then worked for Roland Liccioni at the famed Le Francais restaurant (Wheeling, Illinois), where he started as line cook and worked his way through all stations to become sous chef under Liccioni. David then worked for six years as chef de cuisine of Sanford restaurant in Milwaukee. David created Braise on the Go Traveling Culinary School in the summer of 2004. In 2008, he launched Braise RSA (restaurant supported agriculture), which brings locally sourced foods into local restaurants. His most recent accomplishment is the opening of Braise Restaurant and Culinary School in December of 2011. From this endeavor came 2013 and 2014 James Beard Award nominations for Best Chef: Midwest.

Michelle Tam (page 47)

Michelle Tam is the food nerd and working mom behind *Nom Nom Paleo*, a popular food blog that was recognized by *Saveur* magazine as the world's Best Special Diets Food Blog in 2012. Along with her husband, Henry Fong, Michelle wrote a cookbook, *Nom Nom Paleo: Food for Humans*, which became a *New York Times* bestseller. Michelle also created the Webby Award–winning *Nom Nom Paleo* iPad cooking app, one of the App Store's all-time bestselling food and drink apps. Michelle earned a bachelor of science degree in nutrition and food science from the University of California, Berkeley, and a doctorate of pharmacy from the University of California, San Francisco. Along with her husband and two young sons, she lives (to eat!) in Palo Alto, California.

Connie Tran (pages 2 and 30)

Connie Tran got her first experience in the kitchens of her uncle's chain of Orange County restaurants called Seafood Paradise, where she learned wok-style cooking and the grind of a high-speed, high-volume kitchen. Connie teamed up with her mother to open a pan–East Asian restaurant, Cafe D'Orient, where she worked while receiving her master's in East Asian literature. She was hired by famed chef/restaurateur Zov Karamardian at her namesake Zov's Bistro, where she worked for nine years before gaining experience under Michelin-starred Alfred Prasad at Tamarind in London and Stan Ota at Takami Sushi & Robota in Los Angeles. Since opening BEP Vietnamese Kitchen in 2013, Tran has garnered strong press and media attention for her food, and she's made appearances on *Chopped* and *MasterChef* as well as at the Lucky Rice Festival and the LA Wine Fest. To attend BEP Vietnamese Kitchen pop-up dinners, sign up to be on the waiting list at www.bepkitchen.com

Jason Vincent (page 54)

Jason Vincent's journey began when he was only fifteen, working in a pizza kitchen in Cleveland. After graduating from the Culinary Institute of America in Hyde Park, New York, he spent time in renowned restaurants, including Fore Street in Portland, Maine; Commander's Palace in New Orleans; and Arzak in San Sebastian, Spain. Jason took on his first sous chef role at Lula Cafe in the Logan Square neighborhood of Chicago. In 2009, he opened Nightwood, the Lula Cafe team's new restaurant, as executive chef, where he created a daily-changing menu highlighting Midwestern ingredients, wood-grilled meats, and handmade pasta. A critical favorite, Nightwood won acclaim as Neighborhood Restaurant of the Year in the *Chicago Tribune*'s inaugural food awards. Additionally, Nightwood has held the designation of a Michelin Bib Gourmand (noting best hidden culinary value by the guide) since the guide's inception in Chicago. Other notable mentions include being named Chicago's Best Burger by *Chicago* magazine, selection as one of a *Food & Wine* editor's best breakfast spots in Chicago, and inclusion in the *Bon Appétit*'s restaurant editor's top dishes of 2010. In 2013, Vincent was selected by *Food & Wine* as one of their Best New Chefs. In 2014, he was selected as a James Beard Award semifinalist for Best Chef: Great Lakes.

Quealy Watson (page 41)

A San Antonio resident by way of New Orleans, Watson entered the restaurant industry as a dishwasher at Koi Kawa, a local Japanese restaurant, and never left. Over the next couple of years, he worked his way up to kitchen manager at Koi Kawa, then went on to take a job at the classic French Bistro Vatel, followed by the upscale Oloroso. Like many chefs at the time, Watson had become obsessed with modernist techniques, so when he heard about a guy opening a restaurant in San Antonio with a sous vide setup, he jumped at the opportunity to become involved. That guy turned out to be Chad Carey, and the restaurant was The Monterey. In a matter of months, Watson went from sous chef to head chef. After four years at The Monterey, Watson and Carey started working on the concept for Hot Joy, which took Watson back to his Asian cooking roots. This time, it wasn't just Japanese, but also Thai, Sichuan, and even Mongolian influences. After operating Hot Joy as a successful pop-up at The Monterey for nine months, they found a permanent location, and Hot Joy opened in 2014 with Watson as chef and partner.

David Welch (page 93)

While David Welch has spent the better part of his adulthood working in some of Portland's finest restaurants, such as Wildwood and Carafe, he split his time following his passion for journalism. He has served as a reporter for Oregon Public Broadcasting and a producer for *The Savvy Traveler* radio show, as well as lent his expertise to national radio programs like NPR's *Morning Edition*, *Weekend Edition*, *Day to Day*, American Public Media's *Marketplace*, *Weekend America*, and the popular food show *The Splendid Table*. Welch has also penned stories for a number of local publications, including *Portland Monthly*, the *Oregonian*, and *Edible Portland*. At Lincoln and Sunshine Tavern, Welch has curated a wine list that runs the gamut from star Oregon pinots to gavi grown near the Ligurian border. His playful cocktails are seasonally focused concoctions rooted in the classics. His ever-changing drink menus are enhanced with an array of house-made sodas, including rosemary-grapefruit and blood orange–vanilla, in addition to handpicked import brews and microbrews.

Jasper White (page 16)

Jasper White was born in New Jersey in 1954, and he spent much of his childhood on a farm near the Jersey Shore. Crediting his love of good food to his Italian grandmother, Jasper began his cooking career in 1973, after graduating from the Culinary Institute of America, and worked at restaurants in New York, Florida, California, Washington state, and Montana. In 1983, Jasper's Restaurant opened on Boston's historic waterfront. Both chef and restaurant received numerous awards and were featured extensively in national and local media. In 1990, Jasper was given the James Beard Award for Best Chef: Northeast. In 2000, Jasper surprised people who thought he was inextricably linked to fine dining when he opened Jasper White's Summer Shack in Cambridge, Massachusetts. The success of the first restaurant has spawned three more Summer Shacks at Mohegan Sun Casino in Connecticut; Boston's Back Bay; and Dedham, Massachusetts. From their inception, the Summer Shacks have received enthusiastic reviews from local and national press, including the 2001 James Beard Award nomination for Best New Restaurant. In addition to his restaurants, Jasper is also a partner in Georges Bank, LLC, a wholesale seafood company in South Boston that specializes in supplying the freshest, most sustainable "boat-to-table" fish and shellfish available.

Andrew Zimmerman (page 61)

Since taking the culinary lead at Sepia in 2009, Chef Andrew Zimmerman has garnered national acclaim for his inventive American cuisine. His creative direction in the kitchen has earned the Chicago restaurant a Michelin star since 2011. Zimmerman was invited to cook at the James Beard House in New York City in 2010. He's received a James Beard Award nomination for Best Chef: Great Lakes in 2012, 2013, and 2014, and StarChefs.com chose him as a 2011 Rising Star Chef. For the 2011–2013 Jean Banchet Awards, he was nominated as Chef of the Year, and Sepia won as Restaurant of the Year in 2012. In September 2012, Zimmerman successfully defeated Iron Chef Marc Forgione on Food Network's *Iron Chef America* in Battle Cream Cheese. In addition to the culinary recognition, the chef has been honored for his community involvement, receiving the 2012 Humanitarian of the Year award from *Plate* magazine. He was also invited by State Department Chief of Protocol Capricia Penavic Marshall to join the newly formed American Chef Corps to serve the country in a diplomatic capacity. Zimmerman joins the ranks of other nationally renowned chefs to showcase American cuisine to other nations, enhance formal diplomacy, and cultivate cultural understanding.

Andrew Zimmern (pages 14 and 86)

Andrew Zimmern is a chef, writer, and teacher as well as the creator, host, and co-executive producer of the Travel Channel's *Bizarre Foods with Andrew Zimmern*, *Andrew Zimmern's Bizarre World*, and *Bizarre Foods America*. Zimmern is a six-time nominee and three-time James Beard Award winner for Best Television Personality/Host and Best Television Program on Location. His MSN.com web series, Toyota's *Appetite for Life*, received an Effie in 2010. *Go Fork Yourself with Andrew Zimmern and Molly Mogren* won the Stitcher Award for Best Food/Cooking Podcast in 2012, and AndrewZimmern.com has been nominated for the last two years for Best Food Website by the Webby Awards. Zimmern is a contributing editor at *Food & Wine* magazine, a columnist at *Mpls.St.Paul* magazine, and a senior editor at *Delta Sky* magazine. He is the author of *The Bizarre Truth*, *Andrew Zimmern's Bizarre World of Food,* and *Andrew Zimmern's Field Guide to Exceptionally Weird, Wild & Wonderful Foods*. Zimmern's food truck, Andrew Zimmern's Canteen, debuted in the summer of 2012. The menu showcases inspired versions of food he's discovered on the road, from Nicaraguan dulce de leche shaved ice to the *cabrito* sausage grinders made with an exclusive all-natural goat blend from Pat LaFrieda Meat Purveyors.

Cesar Zapata (page 87)

Bursting onto Miami's culinary scene in 2010 with Blue Piano, Cesar Zapata gained notoriety for his über-craveable "haute stoner food," served at the late-night wine bar and live music locale owned and operated with partner Aniece Meinhold. But it was his next venture that placed him on the culinary map with the city's first official pop-up restaurant, Phuc Yea! An intimate graffiti and hip-hop shop turning out Zapata's killer twists on southern Vietnamese street food—as well as classic dishes hailing from Meinhold's mother's family recipes—the restaurant quickly amassed a cultlike following by virtue of Zapata's deft touch. After the planned three-month reign, and much to the dining public's dismay, Phuc Yea! closed its doors, and Zapata and Meinhold sprung full-fledge into their current venture: The Federal, Food, Drinks & Provisions. After more than a decade behind the range at numerous prestigious establishments, Zapata calls The Federal home, racking up local and national attention for his unconventional and amazingly satisfying riff on classic Americana cuisine. Aside from his duties as chef/owner at The Federal, Zapata serves as executive chef of the Pious Pig Restaurant Group and is working on the highly anticipated relaunch of Phuc Yea!

METRIC CONVERSIONS AND EQUIVALENTS

APPROXIMATE METRIC EQUIVALENTS

Volume

¼ teaspoon	1 milliliter
½ teaspoon	2.5 milliliters
¾ teaspoon	4 milliliters
1 teaspoon	5 milliliters
1¼ teaspoon	6 milliliters
1½ teaspoon	7.5 milliliters
1¾ teaspoon	8.5 milliliters
2 teaspoons	10 milliliters
1 tablespoon (½ fluid ounce)	15 milliliters
2 tablespoons (1 fluid ounce)	30 milliliters
¼ cup	60 milliliters
⅓ cup	80 milliliters
½ cup (4 fluid ounces)	120 milliliters
⅔ cup	160 milliliters
¾ cup	180 milliliters
1 cup (8 fluid ounces)	240 milliliters
1¼ cups	300 milliliters
1½ cups (12 fluid ounces)	360 milliliters
1⅔ cups	400 milliliters
2 cups (1 pint)	460 milliliters
3 cups	700 milliliters
4 cups (1 quart)	0.95 liter
1 quart plus ¼ cup	1 liter
4 quarts (1 gallon)	3.8 liters

Length

⅛ inch	3 millimeters
¼ inch	6 millimeters
½ inch	1¼ centimeters
1 inch	2½ centimeters
2 inches	5 centimeters
2 ½ inches	6 centimeters
4 inches	10 centimeters
5 inches	13 centimeters
6 inches	15¼ centimeters
12 inches (1 foot)	30 centimeters

Weight

¼ ounce	7 grams
½ ounce	14 grams
¾ ounce	21 grams
1 ounce	28 grams
1¼ ounces	35 grams
1½ ounces	42.5 grams
1⅔ ounces	45 grams
2 ounces	57 grams
3 ounces	85 grams
4 ounces (¼ pound)	113 grams
5 ounces	142 grams
6 ounces	170 grams
7 ounces	198 grams
8 ounces (½ pound)	227 grams
16 ounces (1 pound)	454 grams
35.25 ounces (2.2 pounds)	1 kilogram

METRIC CONVERSION FORMULAS

To Convert	Multiply
Ounces to grams	Ounces by 28.35
Pounds to kilograms	Pounds by.454
Teaspoons to milliliters	Teaspoons by 4.93
Tablespoons to milliliters	Tablespoons by 14.79
Fluid ounces to milliliters	Fluid ounces by 29.57
Cups to milliliters	Cups by 236.59
Cups to liters	Cups by .236
Pints to liters	Pints by .473
Quarts to liters	Quarts by .946
Gallons to liters	Gallons by 3.785
Inches to centimeters	Inches by 2.54

COMMON INGREDIENTS AND THEIR APPROXIMATE EQUIVALENTS

1 cup uncooked white rice = 185 grams
1 cup all-purpose flour = 140 grams
1 stick butter (4 ounces • ½ cup • 8 tablespoons) = 110 grams
1 cup butter (8 ounces • 2 sticks • 16 tablespoons) = 220 grams
1 cup brown sugar, firmly packed = 225 grams
1 cup granulated sugar = 200 grams

OVEN TEMPERATURES

To convert Fahrenheit to Celsius, subtract 32 from Fahrenheit, multiply the result by 5, then divide by 9.

Description	Fahrenheit	Celsius	British Gas Mark
Very cool	200°	95°	0
Very cool	225°	110°	¼
Very cool	250°	120°	½
Cool	275°	135°	1
Cool	300°	150°	2
Warm	325°	165°	3
Moderate	350°	175°	4
Moderately hot	375°	190°	5
Fairly hot	400°	200°	6
Hot	425°	220°	7
Very hot	450°	230°	8
Very hot	475°	245°	9

Information compiled from a variety of sources, including *Recipes into Type* by Joan Whitman and Dolores Simon (Newton, MA: Biscuit Books, 2000); *The New Food Lover's Companion* by Sharon Tyler Herbst (Hauppauge, NY: Barron's, 1995); and *Rosemary Brown's Big Kitchen Instruction Book* (Kansas City, MO: Andrews McMeel, 1998).

INDEX

A

aek jeot, xii
aged fish sauce, 86
Anchovy Salad, 66–68
appetizers. *See* small bites; vegetables
apple cider gastrique, 52
apples
    Apple Fritters with Fish Sauce Apple Marmalade,
        102–4
    Apple Relish, 8
Armstrong, Govind, 107
Asian Citrus Dressing, 46–47
Avocado Mash, 76–78

B

bánh mi, 42
Barbecue Shrimp Sauce, 10–12
bean sprouts, 72–74
béarnaise, 9
Becerra, Octavio, 113
Bernstein, Michelle, 107
    background on, 105
    Mussels in Coconut Chili Broth, 88–89
Besh, John, 109
beverages. *See* cocktails
Bezaire, Spencer
    background on, 105
    Korean *Pikliz*, 45
BLiS, xii, 86, 102
Bloody Mary, 93
Blue Crab Fried Rice with *Nam Phrik Pla*, 82–83

Boon, Ho Chee
    background on, 105
    Steamed Dover Sole with Fried Chopped Radish in
        Soya Sauce, 80–81
Boulud, Daniel, 112
Braised Duck with Ginger Lime Slaw, 28–29
Brioza, Nicole, 106
Brioza, Stuart
    background on, 105–6
    Rice-Seared Red Trout with Mandarin and Hazelnut
        Brown Butter, 84–85
brisket, 70–71
broth, 16–18
    Mussels in Coconut Chili Broth, 88–89
    Spicy Garlic Ginger Broth, 22
Brussels sprouts, 46–47
Buddha's Hand Ice Cream, 98–101
Bull, David, 112
Burke, David, 112
Burrell, Anne, 106
Bybee, Jeffrey, 109

C

cabbage
    Ginger Lime Slaw, 28–29
    Hamachi Tostada with Fish Sauce Vinaigrette,
        76–78
    Kimchi Stew with Tuna and Ramen Noodles, 19–21
    Korean *Pikliz*, 45
Caesar Dressing, 23–25
Candied Buddha's Hand, 98–101

candied pecans, 30
Candied Shrimp, 26–27
caramel, 87
   Caramel Miso Glaze, 6
   Vietnamese Caramel Chicken, 60
   Sweet and Spicy Caramel Corn with Cashews and
      Fish Sauce Caramel, 32–33
Caramelized Fish Sauce, 44
Carey, Chad, 41, 116
Carmellini, Andrew, 113
Carrot-Pineapple Shrub, 96
cashews, 32–33
chicken
   Chicken and Candied Shrimp Salad, 26–27
   Crab Fat Wings, 40–41
   Thai Hot and Sour Coconut Chicken Soup, 14–15
   Vietnamese Caramel Chicken, 60
Chili Broth, 88–89
Chili Paste, 56–58
Chong, Alexis
   background on, 106
   Blue Crab Fried Rice with *Nam Phrik Pla*, 82–83
chowder. *See* soups
cocktails
   Fish Sauce Bloody Mary, 93
   Hanoi High Five, 94–95
   Saigon Shrub, 96
coconut
   Coconut Buddha's Hand Sundae with Fish Sauce
      Latik, 98–101
   Coconut Chili Broth, 88–89
   Thai Hot and Sour Coconut Chicken Soup, 14–15
Cohen, Leah
   background on, 106
   Vietnamese Meatballs, 39
colatura di alici, x
crab
   Blue Crab Fried Rice with *Nam Phrik Pla*, 82–83
   Crab and Roasted Tomato Soup in Spicy Garlic
      Ginger Broth, 22
   Crab Fat Wings, 40–41
Craft, Gerard, x
   background on, 107
   Ode to Sardella, 56–58
Crispy Farmer's Market Vegetables with Caramelized
     Fish Sauce, 44
Crispy Pork Steam Buns with Fish Sauce Vinaigrette,
     34–35
Crispy Shallots, 76–78
Crispy Vegetables, 44
croutons, 23–25
Cucumber Relish, 19–20

D

Dady, Jason
   background on, 107
   Shrimp and Pork Belly Bánh Mi, 42
de Cavel, Jean-Robert, 112
dessert
   Apple Fritters with Fish Sauce Apple Marmalade,
      102–4
   Coconut Buddha's Hand Sundae with Fish Sauce
      Latik, 98–101
Dotolo, Vinny
   background on, 107
   Hamachi Tostada with Fish Sauce Vinaigrette,
      76–78
Dover sole, 80–81
dressing, 48–49. *See also* vinaigrette
   Asian Citrus Dressing, 46–47
   Caesar Dressing, 23–25
   Nước Mắm Apple Cider Gastrique, 52
   Spicy Palm Sugar Syrup, 30
   Sriracha Mayo, 39
drinks. *See* cocktails
Dua Gia (Pickled Bean Sprouts), 72–74
duck
   Braised Duck with Ginger Lime Slaw, 28–29
   Spice-Lacquered Duck Breasts, Baby Turnips, and
      Turnip Greens, 61–63
Duplechan, Todd, xi
   background on, 107–8
   Fermented Pork and Rice Sausage, Larb Salad, and
      Fish Sauce Vinaigrette, 64–65

E

Eagan, Bridget, 112
eggs
   Fermented Pork and Rice Sausage, Larb Salad, and
      Fish Sauce Vinaigrette, 64–65
   Thit Kho Caramelized Braised Pork Belly and Eggs,
      72–74

F

Faber, Kresha
   background on, 108
   Homemade Fish Sauce, 4
Falk, David, 112
Fermented Pork and Rice Sausage, Larb Salad, and
     Fish Sauce Vinaigrette, 64–65
fish. *See* seafood
fish sauce
   aged fish sauce, 86
   as blood of Vietnamese cooking, xv–xvi
   brands, xii–xiii
   Caramelized Fish Sauce, 44

Fish Sauce Apple Marmalade, 102–4
Fish Sauce Béarnaise, 9
Fish Sauce Bloody Mary, 93
Fish Sauce Caramel, 32–33, 87
Fish Sauce Latik, 98–101
Fish Sauce Vinaigrette, 34–35, 50–51, 64–65, 76–78
history, x
making, x–xii
salt content in, xv
selecting, xii
storage, xv
Underbelly Fish Sauce, 44
Vietnamese terminology, xv
Zucchini Tofu Shrimp Frittata with Fish Sauce, 90
fish sauce, homemade
Homemade Fish Sauce, 4
Vegan *Nước Chấm*, 2–3
Five Crabs, xiii
Flying Lion, xiii
Fong, Henry, 115
Ford, Benjamin, 107
Forgione, Marc, 117
Freedmen's Pulled Pork, 69
fried rice, 82–83
frittata, 90
fritters, 102–4
Fuchs, Karl-Josef, 109
Fultineer, Dylan
    background on, 108
    Rappahannock Mignonette, 7

G
garum, x, xi
gastrique, 52
Gaudet, Matthew
    background on, 108
    Marinated Grilled Short Rib with Anchovy Salad,
        Green Tomato Jam, and Sweet Potato Purée,
        66–68
Gelburd-Kimler, Alexis, 108
Gilmore, Jack
    background on, 108–9
    Kimchi Stew with Tuna and Ramen Noodles, 19–21
ginger
    Braised Duck with Ginger Lime Slaw, 28–29
    Crab and Roasted Tomato Soup in Spicy Garlic
        Ginger Broth, 22
    Ginger Lime Slaw, 28–29
    Ginger Lime Vinaigrette, 28–29
glazes
    Caramel Miso Glaze, 6
    Duck Glaze, 61–63
Goin, Suzanne, 108
Gourdet, Gregory, 16

Green Mango, Sorrel, and Candied Pecans in Spicy
    Palm Sugar Syrup, 30
Green Tomato Jam, 66–68
greens
    Skillet Greens, Crisp Shallots, *Nước Mắm* Apple
        Cider Gastrique, 52
    Spice-Lacquered Duck Breasts, Baby Turnips, and
        Turnip Greens, 61–63
Grilled Peaches, Crispy Maine Shrimp, Chiles, and
    Herbs, 79
Gulotta, Michael
    background on, 109
    MoPho-Style Barbecue Shrimp Sauce, 10–12

H
Halibut with Browned Butter, Lemon, and Aged Fish
    Sauce, 86
Hamachi Tostada with Fish Sauce Vinaigrette, 76–78
Hanoi High Five, 94–95
Harvey, Laurie Sheddan
    background on, 109
    Hanoi High Five, 94–95
Hazelnut Brown Butter, 84–85
Hogan, John, 106
Homemade Fish Sauce, 4
Hopkins, Gina, 109
Hopkins, Linton
    background on, 109
    Skillet Greens, Crisp Shallots, *Nước Mắm* Apple
        Cider Gastrique, 52
hot and sour coconut chicken soup (*tom kha gai*),
    14–15
Humm, Daniel, 106
Hung, Michael
    background on, 110
    Wood Roasted Summer Squash with Palm Sugar,
        Soy, and Fish Sauce Vinaigrette, 50–51

I
ice cream, 98–101
Ikeda, Kikunae, x
Izard, Stephanie
    Apple Relish, 8
    background on, 110

J
jam, 66–68. *See also* marmalade
Jennings, Kate, 110
Jennings, Matt
    background on, 110
    Grilled Peaches, Crispy Maine Shrimp, Chiles, and
        Herbs, 79
Joho, Jean, 108

K

Kaffir Lemongrass Chicken, 26–27
Kahan, Paul, 108
Kale Caesar Salad with Spiedini Croutons, 23–25
Kamm, Tom, 109
Karamardian, Zov, 116
Katz, Sandor, ix, xi
Keller, Loretta, 114
Kim, Edward
    background on, 110–11
    Chicken and Candied Shrimp Salad, 26–27
Kimchi Stew with Tuna and Ramen Noodles, 19–21
Kluger, Dan, 108
Koketsu, Craig, 114
Korean *Pikliz*, 45
Krasinski, Nicole, 85
Kritzer, Amy
    background on, 111
    Mustard and Beer-Braised Brisket, 70–71

L

Lancaster, Dustin, 105
Larb Salad, 64–65
Late Summer Pasta Sauce, 54–55
latik, 98–101
Lee, Ed, 86
Lee, Jiyeon
    background on, 111
    Zucchini Tofu Shrimp Frittata with Fish Sauce, 90
Lefebvre, Ludo, 107
Leonard, Mary Helen
    background on, 111
    Crab and Roasted Tomato Soup in Spicy Garlic
      Ginger Broth, 22
LeRoy, Evan, ix
    background on, 111
    Freedmen's Pulled Pork, 69
Lewis, Andrew, ix
    Apple Fritters with Fish Sauce Apple Marmalade,
      102–4
    background on, 111–12
Liccioni, Roland, 115
Lieb, Jeremy
    background on, 112
    Fish Sauce Béarnaise, 9
Lin, Mei
    background on, 112
    Vietnamese Caramel Chicken, 60
Lobster with Fish Sauce Caramel, 87
Louis, Jenn, 93
Luzande, Kevin
    background on, 112–13
    Shrimp Toast with *Nước Chấm*, 36–38

M

Maher, Jessica, 107
mango, 30
Marinated Grilled Short Rib with Anchovy Salad,
    Green Tomato Jam, and Sweet Potato Purée,
    66–68
marmalade, 102–4
Martinez, David, 105
meat entrées
    Fermented Pork and Rice Sausage, Larb Salad, and
      Fish Sauce Vinaigrette, 64–65
    Freedmen's Pulled Pork, 69
    Marinated Grilled Short Rib with Anchovy Salad,
      Green Tomato Jam, and Sweet Potato Purée,
      66–68
    Mustard and Beer-Braised Brisket, 70–71
    Spice-Lacquered Duck Breasts, Baby Turnips, and
      Turnip Greens, 61–63
    Thit Kho Caramelized Braised Pork Belly and Eggs,
      72–74
    Vietnamese Caramel Chicken, 60
meatballs, 39
Meewes, Veronica
    background on, 113
    Kale Caesar Salad with Spiedini Croutons, 23–25
Megachef, xiii, 64, 82
mignonette, 7
Militello, Mark, 107
MilkCare Foundation, xvi
Mina, Michael, 106
miso glaze, 6
mocktail, 96
MoPho-Style Barbecue Shrimp Sauce, 10–12
Moss, Elliott, 114
Mussels in Coconut Chili Broth, 88–89
Mustard and Beer-Braised Brisket, 70–71

N

Nam Phrik Pla, 82–83
nam pla, xii
Nieporent, Drew, 106
Nixon, Lara, ix
    background on, 113
    Saigon Shrub, 96
noodles. *See* pasta; ramen noodles
nước chấm, xv, xvi. *See also* Vegan *Nước Chấm*
    Shrimp Toast with *Nước Chấm*, 36–38
nước mắm, xii, xv
    Nước Mắm Apple Cider Gastrique, 52
nước mắm nguyên chất, xv
nước mắm pha, xv

nuts
    Green Mango, Sorrel, and Candied Pecans in Spicy
        Palm Sugar Syrup, 30
    Hazelnut Brown Butter, 84–85
    Sweet and Spicy Caramel Corn with Cashews and
        Fish Sauce Caramel, 32–33

O

Ode to Sardella, 56–58
One Crab, xiii
Ortiz, Rene, 106
Ota, Stan, 116

P

palm sugar, 30, 50–51
Pandel, Chris, x
    background on, 113
    Shaved Winter Squash, 48–49
Passot, Roland, 110
pasta, 56–58
pasta sauce, 54–55
patis, xii
peaches, 79
pecans, 30
Pera, Ryan, x
    background on, 113–14
    Braised Duck with Ginger Lime Slaw, 28–29
Pettry, Annie
    background on, 114
    Sweet and Spicy Caramel Corn with Cashews and
        Fish Sauce Caramel, 32–33
Pham, Hong
    background on, 114
    Thit Kho Caramelized Braised Pork Belly and Eggs,
        72–74
Pham, Kim
    background on, 114
    Thit Kho Caramelized Braised Pork Belly and Eggs,
        72–74
Phu Quoc, xii, xiii
pickles/pickling
    Dua Gia (Pickled Bean Sprouts), 72–74
    Kimchi Stew with Tuna and Ramen Noodles, 19–21
    Korean *Pikliz*, 45
pikliz, 45
pineapple, 96
Pollin, Pierre, 115
Pope, Monica
    background on, 114
    Caramel Miso Glaze, 6
pork
    Crispy Pork Steam Buns with Fish Sauce
        Vinaigrette, 34–35

Fermented Pork and Rice Sausage, Larb Salad, and
    Fish Sauce Vinaigrette, 64–65
Freedmen's Pulled Pork, 69
Vietnamese Meatballs, 39
pork belly
    Shrimp and Pork Belly Bánh Mi, 42
    Thit Kho Caramelized Braised Pork Belly and Eggs,
        72–74
Pork Sauce, 69
prahoc, xii
Prasad, Alfred, 116
Puck, Wolfgang, 60, 112
Pyle, Stephan, 112

R

ramen noodles, 19–21
Rappahannock Mignonette, 7
Red Boat, xii, 66, 85, 86, 93
relish
    Apple Relish, 8
    Cucumber Relish, 19–20
rice
    Blue Crab Fried Rice with *Nam Phrik Pla*, 82–83
    Fermented Pork and Rice Sausage, Larb Salad, and
        Fish Sauce Vinaigrette, 64–65
    Rice-Seared Red Trout with Mandarin and Hazelnut
        Brown Butter, 84–85
Richman, Alan, 108
Ross, John, 113

S

Saigon Shrub, 96
salad. *See also* slaw
    Anchovy Salad, 66–68
    Chicken and Candied Shrimp Salad, 26–27
    Ginger Lime Slaw, 28–29
    Green Mango, Sorrel, and Candied Pecans in Spicy
        Palm Sugar Syrup, 30
    Kale Caesar Salad with Spiedini Croutons, 23–25
    Larb Salad, 64–65
salt content, in fish sauce, xv
Samuelsson, Marcus, 60, 108, 112
sardella, 56–58
sauce. *See also* fish sauce; relish
    Caramel Miso Glaze, 6
    Fish Sauce Béarnaise, 9
    fish sauce in, 6–12
    Hazelnut Brown Butter, 84–85
    Late Summer Pasta Sauce, 54–55
    MoPho-Style Barbecue Shrimp Sauce, 10–12
    Pork Sauce, 69
    Rappahannock Mignonette, 7
sausage, 64–65

seafood
    Blue Crab Fried Rice with *Nam Phrik Pla*, 82–83
    Grilled Peaches, Crispy Maine Shrimp, Chiles, and Herbs, 79
    Halibut with Browned Butter, Lemon, and Aged Fish Sauce, 86
    Hamachi Tostada with Fish Sauce Vinaigrette, 76–78
    Kimchi Stew with Tuna and Ramen Noodles, 19–21
    Lobster with Fish Sauce Caramel, 87
    Mussels in Coconut Chili Broth, 88–89
    Rice-Seared Red Trout with Mandarin and Hazelnut Brown Butter, 84–85
    Seafood Chowder with Thai Flavors, 16–18
    Shrimp and Pork Belly Bánh Mi, 42
    Steamed Dover Sole with Fried Chopped Radish in Soya Sauce, 80–81
    Zucchini Tofu Shrimp Frittata with Fish Sauce, 90
Sedlar, John, 112
shallots
    Hamachi Tostada with Fish Sauce Vinaigrette, 76–78
    Skillet Greens, Crisp Shallots, *Nước Mắm* Apple Cider Gastrique, 52
Shaved Winter Squash, 48–49
Shepherd, Chris
    background on, 114–15
    Crispy Farmer's Market Vegetables with Caramelized Fish Sauce, 44
Shook, Jon
    background on, 107
    Hamachi Tostada with Fish Sauce Vinaigrette, 76–78
short ribs, 66–68
shottsuru, xii
shrimp
    Chicken and Candied Shrimp Salad, 26–27
    Grilled Peaches, Crispy Maine Shrimp, Chiles, and Herbs, 79
    MoPho-Style Barbecue Shrimp Sauce, 10–12
    Shrimp and Pork Belly Bánh Mi, 42
    Shrimp Toast with *Nước Chấm*, 36–38
    Zucchini Tofu Shrimp Frittata with Fish Sauce, 90
shrub, 96
side dishes. See small bites; vegetables
Skillet Greens, Crisp Shallots, *Nước Mắm* Apple Cider Gastrique, 52
slaw
    Braised Duck with Ginger Lime Slaw, 28–29
    Hamachi Tostada with Fish Sauce Vinaigrette, 76–78
    Warm Brussels Sprout Slaw with Asian Citrus Dressing, 46–47

small bites
    Crab Fat Wings, 40–41
    Crispy Pork Steam Buns with Fish Sauce Vinaigrette, 34–35
    Shrimp and Pork Belly Bánh Mi, 42
    Shrimp Toast with *Nước Chấm*, 36–38
    Sweet and Spicy Caramel Corn with Cashews and Fish Sauce Caramel, 32–33
    Vietnamese Meatballs, 39
sole, 80–81
Sorenson, Corey
    background on, 115
    Coconut Buddha's Hand Sundae with Fish Sauce Latik, 98–101
Sorenson, Tim
    background on, 115
    Coconut Buddha's Hand Sundae with Fish Sauce Latik, 98–101
sorrel, 30
soups. *See also* broth
    Crab and Roasted Tomato Soup in Spicy Garlic Ginger Broth, 22
    Kimchi Stew with Tuna and Ramen Noodles, 19–21
    Seafood Chowder with Thai Flavors, 16–18
    Thai Hot and Sour Coconut Chicken Soup, 14–15
soya sauce, 80–81
Spice-Lacquered Duck Breasts, Baby Turnips, and Turnip Greens, 61–63
Spiedini Croutons, 23–25
sprouts. *See* bean sprouts
squash. *See* summer squash; winter squash
Squid brand, xiii, 9, 28
Sriracha Mayo, 39
Steam Buns, 34–35
Steamed Dover Sole with Fried Chopped Radish in Soya Sauce, 80–81
Stone, Larry, 106
summer squash, 50–51
Swanson, David
    background on, 115
    Crispy Pork Steam Buns with Fish Sauce Vinaigrette, 34–35
Sweet and Spicy Caramel Corn with Cashews and Fish Sauce Caramel, 32–33
Sweet Potato Purée, 66–68
Symon, Michael, 60, 112

T

Tam, Michelle
    background on, 115
    Warm Brussels Sprout Slaw with Asian Citrus Dressing, 46–47
Tamago, 64–65
Tarragon Vinegar Reduction, 9

Taylor, Cody, 90, 111
Thai dishes
    Thai Hot and Sour Coconut Chicken Soup, 14–15
    Thai Syrup, 94–95
    Thai-Infused Green Chartreuse, 94–95
Thit Kho Caramelized Braised Pork Belly and Eggs, 72–74
Thompson, Troy, 112
Three Crabs, xii–xiii, 8, 28, 60, 90
Tiparos, xiii
Toasted Coconut, 98–101
tofu, 90
tom kha gai (hot and sour coconut chicken soup), 14–15
tomatoes
    Crab and Roasted Tomato Soup in Spicy Garlic Ginger Broth, 22
    Green Tomato Jam, 66–68
Top Chef, 16, 60, 106, 110, 112, 114
tostadas, 76–78
Tramonto, Rick, 113
Tran, Connie, xv–xvi
    background on, 115–16
    Green Mango, Sorrel, and Candied Pecans in Spicy Palm Sugar Syrup, 30
    Vegan *Nước Chấm*, 2–3
trout, 84–85
tuna, 19–21
turnips, 61–63

U
umami, ix, x, 4, 9, 15, 22, 26, 34, 39, 41, 50, 52, 61, 66, 69, 85, 87

V
Vegan *Nước Chấm*, 2–3
vegetables. *See also* salad
    Crispy Farmer's Market Vegetables with Caramelized Fish Sauce, 44
    Korean *Pikliz*, 45
    Shaved Winter Squash, 48–49
    Skillet Greens, Crisp Shallots, *Nước Mắm* Apple Cider Gastrique, 52
    Warm Brussels Sprout Slaw with Asian Citrus Dressing, 46–47
    Wood Roasted Summer Squash with Palm Sugar, Soy, and Fish Sauce Vinaigrette, 50–51
Viet Huong Fish Sauce Company, xii, xiii

Vietnamese
    cooking, xv–xvi
    terminology, xv
    Vietnamese Caramel Chicken, 60
    Vietnamese Meatballs, 39
vinaigrette
    Fish Sauce Vinaigrette, 34–35, 50–51, 64–65, 76–78
    Ginger Lime Vinaigrette, 28–29
    Tarragon Vinegar Reduction, 9
Vincent, Jason
    background on, 116
    Late Summer Pasta Sauce, 54–55
Voltaggio, Michael, 112

W
Warm Brussels Sprout Slaw with Asian Citrus Dressing, 46–47
Waters, Phillip, 113
Watson, Quealy
    background on, 116
    Crab Fat Wings, 40–41
Waxman, Jonathan, 113
Weber, Morgan, 113, 114
Welch, David
    background on, 116–17
    Fish Sauce Bloody Mary, 93
White, Jasper
    background on, 117
    Seafood Chowder with Thai Flavors, 16–18
wings, 40–41
winter squash, 48–49
Wood Roasted Summer Squash with Palm Sugar, Soy, and Fish Sauce Vinaigrette, 50–51

Z
Zapata, Cesar
    background on, 118
    Lobster with Fish Sauce Caramel, 87
Zimmerman, Andrew
    background on, 117
    Spice-Lacquered Duck Breasts, Baby Turnips, and Turnip Greens, 61–63
Zimmern, Andrew
    background on, 117–18
    Halibut with Browned Butter, Lemon, and Aged Fish Sauce, 86
    Thai Hot and Sour Coconut Chicken Soup, 14–15
Zucchini Tofu Shrimp Frittata with Fish Sauce, 90

The **FISH SAUCE** Cookbook

Andrews McMeel Publishing, LLC
an Andrews McMeel Universal company
1130 Walnut Street, Kansas City, Missouri 64106

www.andrewsmcmeel.com

15 16 17 18 19 SDB 10 9 8 7 6 5 4 3 2 1

ISBN: 978-1-4494-6869-9

Library of Congress Control Number: 2015936077

Photographer: Clare Barboza
Food stylist: Julie Hopper
Food stylist assistant: Milana Zettel
Editor: Jean Z. Lucas
Designer: Holly Ogden
Art director: Tim Lynch
Production manager: Carol Coe
Production editor: Maureen Sullivan
Demand planner: Sue Eikos

Page 4: Excerpted from *The DIY Pantry* by Kresha Faber. Copyright © 2014 by F+W Media, Inc. Used by permission of the publisher. All rights reserved.

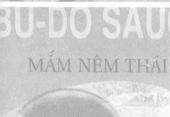